First published in 2019 by David Tucker.

eBook ISBN: 978-1-9161444-0-8
Print ISBN: 9781070812793

Cover design by red heart design
www.redheartdesign.com
Maps and illustrations by Katy Frost
www.bobsyourauntydesign.blogspot.com

Contact David Tucker at www.davidtucker.online
or https://www.facebook.com/davidmarktucker

'You gave a wide place for my steps under me, and my feet did not slip.' Psalm 18:36

To my beloved children - God bless you

September 1995

The evening before the world changed for me, I drank in a pub in Galway with two people I met on the street. Michael was from Cork, had recently moved to Galway but had no roots in the town. Louise had thick black curls and spoke English with a cute French accent that sounded a little nasally, like she had a cold. I was in Ireland doing my best to escape a broken heart and for me, spending time with people I had no history with made it easier to forget my life back home.

Louise told me that she travelled around Ireland for the joy of experiencing something different and had no firm plans on where she went next. I remember putting down my pint and looking over at her as she explained that she may be a little low on money but at least she had a ticket back to France if things got bad.

"Wow that's a good point. How am I going to get back?" I thought.

At that time, I did not know that my return home to the UK would happen in less than twenty-four hours.

The three of us left the pub, not because we were drunk but because our wallets were empty. The sun was gone but there was still a little warmth in the air as we wandered along the seafront to Michael's bedsit paid for by the Irish benefits system. A full moon sat high above an unusually still Atlantic; reflecting a jetty sticking out over the sea. I told my new friends that I thought this was the perfect place to skinny dip.

Michael and I laughed as we removed our clothes.

"Come on Louise, are you joining us?" I asked.

She giggled as she turned around whilst we climbed in.

"Non," she responded simply.

Both Michael and I whooped as the cold and dark waters instantly froze us. We may have had reasons for pride before we climbed in, but as soon as that Atlantic water touched our bits, I am certain they shrunk to the size of an olive and the look of a walnut.

"Come in!" we urged Louise.

At first, she declined and laughed, but after a few minutes she relented and joined us, though I think the swim lasted only a few minutes; any longer and we would have faced a hypothermic incident. As we dried ourselves, Louise went over a short distance to have a modicum of privacy.

"Did you look?" I asked Michael.

"A little," he said and smiled.

There was nothing in this. The three of us had other things in our lives and were more interested in each other's company than anything else.

The following morning, Louise hugged us, said goodbye and made her way to Limerick. Michael and I decided to go to the nearby blues festival that weekend in Clifden.

"What are you going to do after Clifden?" I asked Michael as we waited just outside Galway trying to hitch a ride.

"Well I can't return back here that's for sure," he said as a car passed by.

"Why not?" I asked.

"I spent my housing allowance last night with you two," he responded.

I took a deep breath. "Sounds like two of us are running away for different reasons then."

It was Sunday 10th September 1995 and about midday when a car dropped us off near a small town called Oughtergard. On the journey, I thought about swimming with Louise and her ticket that would take her home. Whilst I had little desire for my adventure to end and would happily have skinny-dipped with many more new friends, I needed to eat. It began to worry me that, unlike Louise, I did not even have a ticket home if things got desperate. I needed money and decided to call Dad in the hope that he could lend me some.

I dialled the number from the pub and my sister answered.

"Hiya Clare – what are you doing there?" I asked.

"Dave! Stay on the line! Have you got enough money to stay on? We have been searching everywhere for you. The police are looking for you and we've had radio adverts asking for information about you. Where are you? Can we call you back?"

"I'm hitching and just stopped at some pub in a place near Galway. Clare what's wrong?"

"You in Ireland? Hold on I'm getting Si."

Simon was my eldest brother. Clare dropped the phone. I heard her screaming for Simon and then heard footsteps as Simon rushed to the phone.

"Dave, are you with anyone?" Simon asked

"Yeah, I'm with a guy called Michael. Si, what is going on?"

"Dave look, Dad was in Victoria station on Monday evening. Unfortunately, he collapsed. A policeman saw him fall and started to do resuscitation."

I felt my knees beginning to go. "So where is he now?" I paused. "Is he dead?"

I heard my brother take a deep breath.

"I'm afraid he is," Simon said.

On the plane back to the UK, I thought about swimming naked with friends the previous evening and how right it seemed at the time. The memory gave me comfort. I thought about my Dad and the last time I spoke with him. I remembered we talked about the previous summer and my adventure in France when I slept underneath the Eiffel Tower. He told me about his dream of leaving the prison service and moving to the Lake District to write books about Christian theology when he retired. Writing was going to be his adventure. Now his life was over that adventure would never happen.

As the plane landed at Heathrow, I was determined to not put off my dreams for later like he did, because later may never come.

Dad was only fifty-two when he died, and whilst it felt like I was torn in two, it gave me a very healthy sense of my own mortality. Twenty years after his death, it was partly this sense that drove me to take Mary and my beloved children to Asia. I was not going to wait until I retired to make my dreams a reality and have an adventure, because that time may never come.

Why Asia? Well, I think Asia is one of the most colourful, beautiful, friendly and amazing places on Earth, and I would happily spend my life exploring its joys. Why would I not want to take my family to a place like that?

Though sometimes my children and wife saw things a little differently.

Sri Lanka

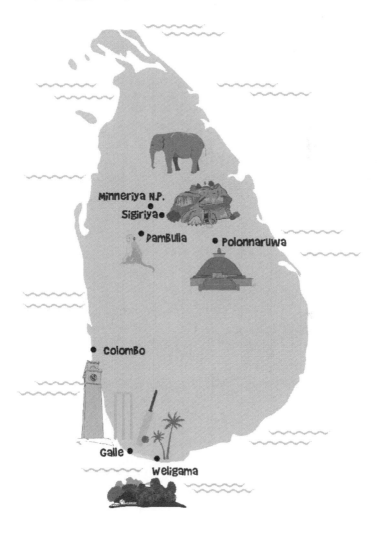

Minneriya N.P.
Sigiriya
DamBulla
Polonnaruwa
ColomBo
Galle
Weligama

Chapter 1: The flight and Digampathana

I had just fallen asleep when Mary hissed at me from across the aisle to wake up. My son Evan was retching over his blanket. Nothing was coming out and, in my fatigue, I irrationally wondered if this was all for show; perhaps some kind of punishment for me. However, this trip to Sri Lanka was my idea and so it was up to me to be positive, to smile and put my arms around him. I wished the journey would just end.

"If only it was just the vomiting," I thought.

This was a dreadful flight. It started to go wrong a few minutes after we took off from London on a plane with personal television screens that either did not turn on or had no reception. Carrie, my eldest child and only daughter, was the first to raise the alarm as she punched at the power button with her thumb.

"Dad I think the TV might be broken," she said.

Her single push quickly turned into a more panicked repetitive thrust. She turned to her brother's TV screen and was marginally relieved to see that her youngest brother's television was also unresponsive. I watched their shoulders fall when they realised that half a day of television was to be replaced by 'dot to dot' books and word searches. This was the reality of buying bargain-basement air tickets.

As we flew over Turkey, I took my youngest son Rueben to the toilet. Rueben was recently toilet trained and needed prompting to go and so I invited him to come with me for a little urinary relief. We stood in the cramped room and discussed the wonders of the light turning on as we locked the door and I explained that after he finished, his outpourings ejected out into space. As I flushed, he instantly screamed; convinced that the toilet would not differentiate the urine from the urinator and that he too was about to be sucked out into the cold night air. I kicked myself for being such a fool for telling him where his waste went. After this incident, every time Mary or I tried to take him to the toilet, he bucked, kicked and screamed like a cornered chimp, and the only way I could get him to the back of the aircraft was to carry him like a rolled-up carpet under my arm. Once near the toilet, the only way we managed to coax him inside was to promise we would not flush and to bribe him with marshmallows.

After seven hours, we disembarked in Kuwait City to catch our flight to Colombo. We took a bus to the plane from the airport terminal, boarded and I 'high fived' the children; thankful that we were on the final leg. My excitement was premature, though, and we sat for an hour on a lifeless plane; cooking in the Middle East heat as we waited for some transferring passengers from Amman. I tried to keep my mind off the discomfort by reading a story about social housing in Kuwait but was brought back to the harsh reality when I looked up to see a cockroach scarper across the drop-down television screen in the aisle.

Evan started his retching a few hours after this.

Finally, we stumbled off the plane in Colombo with children who were so tired that they complained it was hard to walk. Just as we approached the customs hall, all three of them decided they needed the toilet. So, by the time we reached passport control we entered a perfect storm of queues that went back fifty people. Our queue was serviced by the slowest border staff that I have ever encountered, and it took over an hour to get to the front. However, with our passports finally stamped, I looked over to the children.

"Wow kids, we have done it!" I exclaimed, trying to make the flight seem part of a wonderful great adventure, but all I saw was Carrie staring out across space and looking like she may have misplaced her soul. Evan looked at me and promptly burst into tears. This was not quite how I planned the trip would begin.

Whilst I may have been economical on the air tickets, the smartest thing I did on the journey was to book a taxi from the airport to our hotel near the historical centre of Sigiriya. Our driver Buddhika was a young man with a rehearsed speech about Sri Lanka that was loaded with facts about the country. My eyes stung, and I stifled yawns as he told me that schooling for all children had led to a national literacy rate of ninety-two percent, that Sri Lanka has a holiday each full moon, and that green coconuts are for cooking and brown are for drinking.

"When do children leave school?" I asked; feeling obliged to hold the conversation since the children and Mary were almost asleep in the back of the car.

There was a pause.

"Yes," Buddhika answered confidently.

"I mean what age?" I asked again.

"School yes. Children go to school," Buddhika responded.

I realised I had quickly pushed him to the boundaries of his English, and I was too tired to try further and so we drove on in silence.

We drove at a sedate forty kilometres per hour along tree lined avenues. In the early morning, a hazy pink mist clung to the dry paddy fields and mottled sunshine shone through groves of coconut. The ride was very comfortable, but the haze promised that the heat would soon arrive. All along the road, bald dogs slept or patrolled the roadsides. As we drove by, some met our presence with tired indifference whilst others barked furiously. They all appeared to live their lives with their noses a few inches away from the chassis of moving cars.

10

In one town, I saw one rickshaw (called a tuk-tuk) hit a dog and send it somersaulting.

Mary and the children slept for the entire journey. At one point we entered a forest and Buddhika stopped to show the children some monkeys, but we turned around to see Carrie and Evan bent over like rotting stems and Mary snoring with her head back and mouth wide open.

"If only I had a grape to throw into that target," I mentioned to Buddhika and pointed at Mary's mouth.

"Yes, yes. You want grapes?" he asked, eager to please.

We drove for over three hours to get to Sigiriya from the airport. Sri Lanka looked like a small country and I was surprised it took such a long time to travel a distance that was a little wider than my thumb print on my map and a distance that would take a little over an hour in the UK.

My first view of Sigiriya rock was when we were a few minutes away from our hotel. The sandstone monolith punched through the flat horizon. Despite it having the same shape as a wart, I thought it was beautiful. This was a place I had always wanted to see. In my excitement, I woke the children and Mary. They squinted in the bright morning sunlight, stretched and looked miserable.

@@@@@

I knew I was mentally wired to travel the world at the age of eight after the day the Reverend Roger Parkes showed me a picture of the tomb of Jesus. At that time my family attended the local Anglican Church in a small town in the Blue Mountains near Sydney in Australia. Roger Parkes decided to leave us for three months and take a trip of a lifetime to visit all the places he yearned to see. My brother was reading 'the Hobbit' at the time and described the reverend as a modern-day Bilbo Baggins.

On his return, he held a slideshow for the entire congregation and showed us pictures of his travels across Greece, France and Israel. For me, who knew only the sandstone canyons and bushlands around the Blue Mountains, the reverend's slides of Israel were windows into a world that I knew from my regular attendance at church and from the stories in the bible, and the slides of Greece simply astounded me. I never considered that places like Jerusalem and Bethesda existed in the modern world, but there they were displayed onto a screen in full colour. My brothers and sister quickly went off to play with friends in the church grounds. However, I was hooked as he showed us pictures of the Eiffel Tower, the Acropolis, vineyards, the Qumran caves where the Dead Sea Scrolls were found, the reverend wearing a pair of 'Speedos' (lovingly known as budgie smugglers in Australia) floating in the dead sea, the golden Dome of the Rock in Jerusalem, the gnarled olive groves in the Garden of Gethsemane and finally, the simple hewn rock of the Garden Tomb.

"Dad," I whispered, "I'm going to travel the world like the Reverend Roger Parkes."

"Well you will need to work hard at school and get a job," he whispered back.

It took me some time to get going and I blame a move to the UK with my family a year after the reverend's slide show for the delay. However, I never lost that interest in travel and read Jules Verne before bed and watched all the adventures of Jacques Cousteau on his boat in the years before I finally travelled to some of the destinations I dreamt about. Over that period, I had holidays in places like Cornwall and Kent with my family, and I never understood why Dad chose destinations where it always seemed to rain.

Finally, I had my first trip overseas travelling with another church minister who wrote for an evangelical magazine. He asked me to come along to keep his son company on a road trip across Europe to photograph a famous evangelical preacher called Reinhard Bonnke. On that trip, we drove through France, Spain and Portugal to take some photographs of the German evangelist preaching in a park in Lisbon. Once we had the photo, we simply drove back, but the experience left me wanting so much more, not less.

After college, I lived in Paris for a month and slept rough underneath the Eiffel Tower with a crowd of eastern Europeans who travelled to northern Europe after communism collapsed. Shortly after that I met Mary at a cheap vodka night in Middlesbrough in the UK. It was her who got me organised and we travelled around Asia and Australia for a year, and then we cycled around New Zealand because we could not afford any other way to travel. We married and had three children, and whilst Mary was happy for more sedate holidays after children, my wiring was not much changed.

I blame the reverend. It was his slide show that put me on the path that ended up thirty years later in Sri Lanka, with three exhausted children and a wife looking at a rock on the horizon; scowling.

@@@@@

Leaving Buddika's air-conditioned minivan and stepping into the heat of a Sunday morning at our resort left us all instantly dripping in sweat, for we were still dressed for a cold spring morning in the UK. I was the point man on most of the journey and now I shook with tiredness and could barely hold the cold lime juice that the staff brought us to welcome us to the resort. I handed the head role over to Mary and allowed her to manage three bouncing children whose sole focus on arrival was dumping the bags, stripping down and jumping into the

13

pool. Whilst they headed to the pool almost immediately, I fell into a deep sleep in the room and joined them after I woke.

Just as I jumped in, a young Sri Lankan pool attendant appeared in crisp white shorts, a shirt and white towelling socks. He had the look of a 1920s tennis player and made me feel like I had entered the last days of the Raj. We swam as blood-red dragonflies hovered over the water, birds chattered in the trees and butterflies with wings the size of a fifty pence piece fluttered from bush to bush. It was a beautiful setting with the pool overlooked by scrubby bushland and the monolith of Sigiriya rock itself.

We swam, had jumping competitions and races, and played with an inflatable beach ball that Mary had the foresight to pack. Carrie christened the ball 'Andy' after a children's television presenter and, on several occasions, one of us had to sprint across the prickly lawns of the resort; chasing down Andy when he took flight on the hot winds that blew across the grounds. Once I chased Andy down and returned to find Mary working with Evan on his swimming technique. Evan appeared to have the rudiments of breaststroke correct, but for some reason he could only swim backwards, much to her frustration and everyone else's amusement.

Throughout that day, we appeared to be the only guests and treated the pool as our own private property. However, in the late afternoon, a modern coach appeared in the carpark and an army of elderly French package tourists disembarked. They all looked miserable and did not return our smiles as they queued to receive their room keys. Our impression of them did not change, and they continued to look depressed even as they drifted towards the pool for a cooling dip before dinner. With new guests in the pool, Evan and Carrie had enough spatial awareness to leap into water where no one swam.

Rueben, however, had no such caution and leapt over a portly old lady wallowing in the waters wearing sunglasses of a style that were made famous by Jackie Onassis. She looked at my youngest son as if he was a bottled fart she had just opened.

@@@@@

Rueben (my youngest son) has always been full of surprises. He surprised people even before he was born. I remember the first time he surprised me was when Mary interrupted my viewing of a World Cup match between France and Uruguay with a pregnancy stick that showed two solid blue lines. I thought she was just bringing me a cup of tea.

He surprised an old woman in Sri Lanka wearing Jackie Onassis glasses by leaping over her head.

As a toddler he surprised Mary by hiding a small toy and pretending that he had swallowed it. He decided to come clean by pulling the toy out of his nappy only when Mary had a bag packed and was preparing to go to the hospital.

A year before, however, I surprised Rueben. It was a beautiful curling shot that was heading for the top corner of the goal, had Rueben not got in the way. Unfortunately, the ball hit my son just as he lifted his drinking bottle to his mouth. The impact of the ball hitting the cup created a cut so deep that blood poured out from both sides of his mouth. At the hospital, the doctors decided he needed stitches that could only be inserted under a general anaesthetic.

I remember taking Rueben into the operating theatre and cuddling him as they put him to sleep. He was very frightened, but the drugs worked instantly, and he went limp. Only one stitch was required to repair the damage and he was in theatre for less than twenty minutes, but he still needed time in recovery. As he awoke, he looked at me and smiled. I thought he wanted a cuddle. However, as I moved in for an embrace, he outdid the surprise I gave him with the football by giving me a taste of my own medicine and surprising me with a left hook on my lip. He hit me so hard that I needed ice for the swelling.

@@@@@

When the heat of the day disappeared, Mary and I decided that we would take a walk with the children to the nearby village of Digampathana to show them what was outside the walls of the resort, and to purchase a few snacks for our eternally-famished brood. We walked up a dirt road towards the main highway. The road in the evening sunshine turned a delicious pink and initially we walked in solitude, past waxy jungle vines covered in dust. Soon we came to the first houses of the village; breezeblock bungalows set back from the road and painted peppermint green. The baked earth around the houses was swept clean of any foliage.

Evan wandered into the long grass on the road verge and, having lived in Australia, I told him to walk on the road to avoid snakes. Suddenly a moped raced by and, whilst it did not come close to hitting Evan, motherly instinct took over and Mary asked him to walk closer to the verge. The local dogs then became aware of our presence and started yapping as we passed by. To Evan, who was frightened by puppies, being told to walk away from the verge to avoid snakes, then being told to walk closer to the verge to avoid cars and then negotiating baying dogs left him terrified. It was only his prodigious love of food and the promise of a visit to a local store to buy treats that kept him going. He hugged my leg as we walked and refused to look at any of the smiling locals.

It felt like we would never come to the shops as we huddled together for protection and walked gingerly up the street. I was fearful that our experience would end up in a national UK newspaper under a headline like, 'First British citizen in a decade dies of rabies'. However, I had to remain calm for the sake of the children. The residents of Digampathana, dressed in saris or short sleeved shirts and chinos, came to the doors; made aware of our presence by the barking dogs. They smiled and waved at this western freak show walking by. One little girl was playing in the dust, saw us and tore back home. By the time we passed her house, three generations appeared to be waiting on the veranda for our passing. As soon as the youngest toddler saw us, she recoiled in fear and started to scream, much to the amusement of the mother, who promptly picked her up and brought her to Rueben in the hope that they would make friends. The net result was that both Rueben and the little girl screamed at each other in abject fear.

Finally, we came to the shops. They were like the bungalows in the rest of the town except they had glass cases on a veranda, and neat packets of biscuits and swollen packets of crisps stapled onto cardboard that hung from exposed nails. We went into two shops and each time whole families gathered around us to see what we would buy.

"Do you think many people ever leave the resort?" Mary asked as she looked to her side at an old man who stood close to her and leant over the counter.

The old man watched my hand movements with the same interest as he would if I was doing a magic trick, though all I did was pack biscuits and savoury snacks into a cheap plastic bag.

He looked up and smiled at me, "Oh ya kosindra?" he asked.

The word 'kosindra' made me think of a girlfriend I

once had called Kassandra and I had not thought about for years, so I was surprised that of all the places, it was in a shop in Sri Lanka and an old man of Digampathana that reminded me of her.

My knowledge of Sinhalese was limited to a few words and I had no idea at the time what he was asking. I smiled at him.

"Hello!" I said, and then ran out of ideas for anything else to say. This was partly because I was tired and partly because I had my mind on girlfriends from long ago.

When I got home, I searched for what he was asking me.

I think he was asking, "Where are you from?"

Judging by the reaction on our trip to the shops, I am certain the entire town would love to have known the answer.

Chapter 2: Dambulla Caves

It was too hot to walk up the road through Digampathana the following day, and so we took a tuk-tuk to the bus stop on the main road where we sat and waited for the bus to take us to Dambulla. An old man stood on the roadside chatting to other people but, when we turned up, he immediately came over to us. His movement was slow and stiff.

"Hello friend, what country?" he asked, in a voice soaked in mucus.

"England," I responded.

He barely grunted a response and it became apparent that he was not interested in talking with me; it was Rueben with his blonde hair, fair skin and toddler features that really interested him.

"What is your name?" I asked.

He did not look at me.

"Jeewana," he responded after a few moments.

Jeewana tried to interact with Rueben, but the three-year-old turned his back, cuddled into his mum and closed his eyes. I think my son thought that if he kept his eyes closed then the man was simply not there. Jeewana laughed and tried a little harder by touching Rueben's arm gently. Rueben flinched and turned around so that his face was buried tight into his mother. I could see that he was feeling a little overwhelmed and so I decided to diffuse the situation by asking Jeewana about his family.

"Do you have any children?" I asked.

"Yes," he responded. My son is a dentist in Ratnapura."

At that moment Jeewana turned to me and smiled. He looked like he had been chewing on coal. I was so surprised that my next question was out of instinct.

"Does he do your teeth?" I asked.

Jeewana laughed and understood my comment.

"Damage done in younger days," he said.

A bus slowed but did not look like it would stop. Jeewana looked up and moved quickly towards the road.

"This your bus, this your bus!" he said, almost dancing as he waved it down for us. His movement surprised me since moments before, he had approached us with arthritic caution.

The bus that picked us up was a typical South Asian vehicle. It looked like someone had given it a battering with a sledgehammer and the engine sounded like a machine that drives in piles. The only cooling breeze we felt was the displaced air as the crate tore down the road. Every action the bus driver took appeared to be urgent, whether it be revving the engine or braking. I realised why Jeewana had moved so quickly to wave it down; if he was slower it would not have stopped. On a few occasions, we all fell forwards as the driver instigated something akin to an emergency stop to pick up or drop off passengers. The bus driver was clearly in a hurry.

After one stop, a passenger near the back door moved to allow Evan and Rueben to sit down. Rueben immediately fell asleep in this new environment. Mary and I stood, enjoyed the breeze and listened to a man sing a religious cantata with only a tambourine, almost kissing it as he sang. All the locals on the bus studiously ignored the busker and so I took this social cue and did not give any money for a tip and tried to look as nonchalant as I could.

It took ten minutes to reach Dambulla. We should have stayed on the bus a little longer, but we disembarked in the town and realised that we needed to take a tuk-tuk a little further down the road to get us to the caves. However, as we got into the tuk-tuk, Rueben threw a tantrum of a magnitude I have only seen when trying to bath a child with a sore bottom. He screamed because he did not want to sit on my knee and demanded an entire window seat to himself. I think he was in a bad mood because I woke him from his sleep on the bus. However, with the heat and our desire to stop drawing the small crowd that gathered around us to watch a screaming child, we gave in to his demands as it was not too far to travel. Rueben had a significant part of the backseat to himself, Carrie had to sit on my knee and have her legs poking out the door and Evan sat on the driver's knee at the front. If any of us got too close to Rueben's space, he pushed us away like we were pigeons invading his lunch.

At the temple complex, Rueben jumped out of the tuk-tuk, and stood still, with his neck craned, as he stared up at a concrete elephant in the car park.

"What do you think of the elephant Rueben?" I asked.

"I think it looks embarrassed," he responded.

It was true. The statue had rouged-up cheeks to make it look as if it was blushing, or out for a night out on the town.

We crossed a large paved area in front of an enormous Buddhist temple and museum where the main entrance looked like the mouth of a dragon with bulbous and evil eyes. It reminded me of a nightmarish entrance to Chinatown. An enormous Buddha with a peeling chin sat on top of the building. The caves we came to see were hidden behind this statue.

I paid the entrance fee with the expectation that we were nearly at the caves and did not realise that there was a climb up a hill. When the children saw it, they groaned and stepped heavily on to the first step.

"So that Buddha on the building isn't the temple then?" Mary asked.

"Dad I'm tired," Carrie said. "Do we have to go up there?"

"Yeah, Dad," Evan affirmed.

"Rueben I'll carry you," I said, ignoring them all and lifting him onto my shoulders. Carrying a child in that heat was a little like wearing a scarf soaked in vinegar on a summer's day, but there was no other way to get them moving. I knew if I took Rueben then motherly instinct meant that Mary would automatically follow, and the other children would have no choice but to also ascend the hill.

"It's so hot," Mary sighed.

I think she was hoping that I would give up climbing to the caves in the mid-morning heat. We were quickly drenched in sweat. Even though I carried the most weight with Rueben, I was always at the front leading the way. I was certain that Carrie and Evan looked at me in a way that suggested a strong desire to hurl some expletives in my direction even though they were too young to know such language. It was also hard for me to stay polite whilst carrying my son on my shoulders in that heat. I felt sore at them for making the climb feel so much harder with their opposition. Hawkers lined the path and added to my discomfort by trying to sell me Buddha paraphernalia, postcards and cold drinks every few steps.

About halfway up, all the tension and fatigue was suddenly forgotten. Without warning, toque macaques leapt out of the bushes and scarpered across the ground and trees; foraging off the scraps that the pilgrims and the tourists dropped. These monkeys were the size of bed pillows, had hair that made them look like they had bowl head haircuts and had no fear of humans. The children stopped and watched the primates fighting in a tree, and when the argument spilt onto the pathways and came close to Evan and Carrie, they ran up the stairs with a squeal and a laugh. At one point I instinctively put my hand out to usher the children away from the angry primates as I knew they would have no qualm in scratching a child if they got too close. Still, at least it was the monkeys that forced them up the hill and closer to our destination instead of me.

Mary, Carrie, Evan and Rueben looking at the frogs in Dambulla Caves

The caves sat behind a long white pavilion built into the rock overhang. The walls of many of the caves were covered in kaleidoscopic patterns and housed circular stupas and multiple Buddha in the lying or sitting positions. The children had no interest in the statues or the painting but enjoyed looking in the dusty old corners or playing with the net curtains that hid the brooms. In one cave, they discovered an enormous black pot that produced an odd echo and so Mary and I left them grunting and clucking into the cauldron whilst we enjoyed the complex in peace.

After looking in each of the caves, we rested in the shade created by the pavilions even though it gave little respite from the heat. We sat and watched frogs on the lily pads in a pond below us. I thought the caves, the colours and the amazing statues would grab the children's attention, but the reality was that it was the animals of Dambulla that really entertained them. It was a healthy reminder to me that when you are only four foot high, you see the world differently.

Chapter 3: Sigiriya

Migara was an evil man. In a choir of evil men across history, he would be one the best singers; though many people in the audience would not recognise him. When I think about what Migara looked like, I imagine someone who looked like Colonel Gadaffi, but judging by the images of Sri Lankan royalty from this time, I suspect he looked a little more muscular and becoming. Even so, his evil streak compares with many of the world's tyrants. He was a manipulative and sadistic murderer and a wife beater. Ironically, his evil actions led to the building of one of the most famous and beautiful historical sites in Sri Lanka – Sigiriya.

Our villain was born into privilege as the nephew to King Dhatusena. Pictures of the king show him with the chest of a body builder, a metrosexual beard and colourful tunic. To me, he looked like a kind and just master of an important family, though he had his faults. Like many men with power and looks, the king enjoyed the good things that come with such attributes and his first-born son was born by a woman of a lower caste. She named him Kassapya.

Kassapya should have been heir to the throne. However, caste counts with royal bloodlines, and a more suitable woman of a higher caste also bore a son not long after Kassapya was born. This son of the higher caste woman was named Mogallana. Even though Kassapya was older, Mogallana had more blue blood pulsating in his veins and therefore trumped Kassapya as the king-in-waiting.

King Dhatusena was not just a looker and a lover, he was also a visionary builder. He built a large lake called the Kala Wewa near his capital Anuradhapura to provide water for the population and for farming, and when it was full it covered five square miles. After the lake was completed, he turned his attention to building a fifty-four mile canal between the Kala Wewa and another lake with a descent of just one inch per mile for a gentle flow. King Dhatusena was a builder of great and practical things for his subjects to use.

Back to Migara (the villain of the story). Like several famous people such as Charles Darwin, Saddam Hussein and Albert Einstein, Migara married his cousin; the daughter of King Dhatusena. It was soon after the wedding that Migara's malevolence started to show its green shoots, and he regularly hit his new wife with a whip. After one such beating, she ran to her father with bleeding thighs. King Dhatusena was understandably so upset that he summoned Migara into his presence. However, Migara refused to go, and that snub infuriated the king. Perhaps Dhatusena's next action was acting more as an angry father than as a king, and the desire for revenge may have clouded his judgement. If Migara would not stand before him then the king turned on the person that he did have access to. He turned on Migara's mother (his own sister) and barbecued her alive.

Migara was understandably furious with the king. It was Migara who now looked for revenge and he saw an opportunity by befriending Kassapya and sowing seeds of mistrust in Kassapya towards his father. Migara reminded him that it was Kassapya and not Mogallana who was the first born and therefore should be the first in line to be king. On a hunting trip, Migara pushed hard and finally the seed-sowing bore some fruit, and he persuaded Kassapya to have a go at taking the throne.

Our evil man got his revenge, and Kassapya overthrew King Dhatusena in a coup and gave Migara a lot of power. After the murder of his mother, Migara was happy to arrest the former king under Kassapya's authority and paraded him around the royal city as his prisoner.

Architecting the overthrow of the king was not enough for Migara and, just like on the hunting trip, he persuaded Kassapya of the next step he should take. Migara made Kassapaya believe that his imprisoned father had vast wealth hidden near his lake. When Kassapya asked his father about the wealth, he led his son to the edge of the Kala Wewa, the great reservoir he built, dipped his hands in it, turned to his son and said, "this is the only wealth I have."

Kassapya was furious and ordered the execution of his father. Migara's sadistic streak came out again and rather than a quick kill with a sword or a dagger, Migara decided to kill Dhatusena by entombing him alive into a recess in the prison wall.

Even though burning sisters alive and entombing fathers into walls of prison cells seems to be the norm in 500AD for Sri Lankan royals, the locals were not impressed and saw patricide as a very big issue. Kassapya was now king but needed to win over his people. To do this, he invited the Buddhist monks in the area to a party. The monks duly turned up but, as the food was served, they turned their bowls upside down and walked away to show their unhappiness with Kassapya. Feeling unloved and a little threatened, Kassapya decided to move the capital from Anuradhapura to a more remote site in the jungle.

Even though he did not have quite the right levels of royal blood pumping through his veins, he was his father's son and inherited the instinct for engineering. At Sigiriya, King Kasapya made beautiful gardens, irrigation systems, barracks and commercial outbuildings. Above all, he built himself a beautiful palace on top of an enormous sandstone rock. Now, all that is left in Sigiriya are ponds and ruins.

Migara was a villain, but if it was not for his presence in history then the beautiful palace of Sigiriya may never have existed.

@@@@@

The morning air was like kettle steam and simply walking to the dining room for breakfast left our backs damp. If the previous day was stifling, this humidity was another level. After breakfast, we took a tuk-tuk away from Digampathana and towards the sandstone rock of Sigiriya. Everyone we passed waved at us, and nearly all were delighted to see Rueben wave back at them with a vertical hand and a slight twist of a wrist. I have no idea where he learnt how to do it, but it was a perfect royal wave. We drove by houses the colour of bright pink, blue and peppermint green; colours that made them stand out amongst the green of the jungle and scrub around them. The breeze provided a perfect respite to the steaming temperatures and we were all happy.

It was not to last.

I felt excited as I joined the queue for our tickets. There was a sense of keen anticipation amongst all tourists in the line, as if the rock would soon disappear. I got to the front of the line.

"Two adults and three children please," I asked.

"Ninety," a tired voice came through the Perspex window.

Their response confused me as I knew the price was in US dollars.

"Ninety?" I asked.

"Yes."

"What, ninety dollars?" I asked, though I think to the cashier it sounded like an exclamation.

There was a deep sigh from the other side of the

window from the cashier, "Yes."

I was probably not the first person to be surprised by the prices.

"Great, I'm paying ninety dollars to climb a rock," I thought as I paid the money.

My excitement quickly morphed into a deep sense of irritation.

As I approached the family waiting at the ticket entrance, a local man sidled up to me and whispered in my ear as if he was offering drugs. "I carry your child up the rock yes? Very cheap seventy-five dollars yes?"

I was in no mood to accommodate more payouts, particularly when quoted in US dollars. He followed me for several minutes and started to whisper lower prices. I really did want to punch him.

Even before we entered through the main western gate, our t-shirts were soaked in sweat and I felt like I had just wet myself. Again, the same dispiriting fatigue that we experienced in Danbulla set in. Mary insisted on waiting in some scrubby shade by the main path whilst I took Evan and Carrie to a far corner so that I could take a photograph of them away from photobombing tourists. When I returned, she scowled at me in the same way she does when I speak to people for too long at social engagements and she has the job of placating tired children. Sweat beaded on her nose.

"Are you going to take photos the whole time we are here?" she snapped.

In the heat, I took umbrage to her tone.

"No of course not! Though I will not be asking your permission if I do want to take a photograph."

"I was not asking you to ask my permission," she retorted as she stood up to continue the walk.

With her back turned, I grabbed the camera from my pocket, lined up a shot of her legs and bottom, and depressed the shutter button out of spite. Evan and

Rueben looked up at me and smiled, knowing what I just did. They never told their mother that I took the photo, which is good because Mary is never shy of a fight, particularly in the heat.

We carried on up the gentle incline on the main path that bordered the pools that made up the water gardens. These would be full in the monsoon months, but in April they were more like slimy ponds. Bordered by neat grass and ancient brick walls, even the slimy pond water looked temping for a cooling dip. We stopped just before we entered the border garden and drank almost all the water we carried. For the rest of the excursion, only the children would drink.

The path started to climb steeply but it was well maintained. We came to some steep steps and climbed up to a point where we entered a caged spiral staircase that was suspended from a rock face. This was where the toil really began. Carrie and Evan bounded up, and left Mary and I calling their names after their shadows; half begging and half barking. I kept on thinking that the cage would pull away from the rock with Rueben and I inside and wished I could relax and enjoy the view of the landscape and the flat jungle below.

Nerves had the better of me, though, and I hurried on and entered a cave with frescoes of smiling ladies with shrunken midriffs and breasts shaped like swollen champagne flutes. Some say that they are pictures of goddesses; others say they are portraits of Kassapya's harem. Either way, I stood covered in sweat and tried to admire them, but my heart pumped with adrenalin and, since Carrie and Evan were still nowhere to be found, I worried that they had run off the rock and now lay lifeless in the scrub below. I took much greater pleasure in the photos I took of the paintings when I returned to the UK. The painted murals are very beautiful. One thing that I noticed after the fact was that all the women had broad shoulders, like champion swimmers.

We walked along a wrought-iron path suspended in the air and attached to the sandstone rock. At the end, Carrie and Evan stood waiting for us. From then on, the two had no choice; Evan walked close to me and Carrie walked with Mary. After a few minutes of making the children walk according to our middle-aged caution, we came to a plateau that led to the final climb up to the top of the rock. To get to the summit, the final climb was up some metal stairs that ascended a wall of sandstone. Next to the entrance to the stairs was a famous sculpture of a lion's paw. In Kassapya's day, this entrance would have been through the mouth of the lion and walking through it would have been a little like walking into the entrance of a theme park ride.

Evan and the climb up Sigiriya

Despite the height and sheer cliffs around, the guidebooks say that the greatest threat to visitors was the hornets. Not far from the lion's paw was a cage for all to flee to in the event of a swarm. The hornet nests looked like enormous black teeth hanging off the rock. There were signs that requested people kept still and silent in a swarm of wasps. However, I know that if I was in a swarm, I would not stand still and remain calm. I would probably end up running off the rock in a panic and would scream as if someone had rubbed chilli into my undercarriage.

Evan and I began our climb. The stairs looked like old iron scaffolding and a bit transient. Again, I had visions of the stairs tearing away from the rock and us all falling to our deaths in a scene reminiscent of something from 'Final Destination'. For those who have not seen the films, they contain a list of good looking 'b-list' move stars who die in the most astonishing ways such as getting flattened by a bathtub, being hit by an ambulance and falling out a window after having an eye burnt out by a malfunctioning x-ray machine. With these thoughts screaming in my mind, I insisted that Evan walk three steps in front of me and got no closer or further away. I always leant into the rock in an irrational fear that Rueben would fall out of the backpack into which I had him securely strapped.

At the top, Evan and I wandered around ancient brick walls that marked buildings. However, being so physically close to the structures meant we made no sense of anything we looked at. We sat down in the shade to admire the view and I allowed Evan the last dregs of water. As we sat and chatted, three teenage school boys came up to us and asked if Evan would be in a photograph with them. He was so honoured that he stood with his chest puffed out and his chin up whilst I took photos on their mobile phones and on my camera.

"Sri Lankans really are nice people," Evan stated after they left.

The invitation was a confidence boost after the welcome he received from the baying dogs of Digampathana.

Heading down the rock was even worse than the climb up because the stairs disappeared out of view as they turned around a bend and gave me the uncomfortable feeling that I was stepping off into mid-air. All my fears of falling were exacerbated because the crowds coming up appeared to have the urgency and joy of a crowd at the opening of the New Year sales. Regularly pressed against the thin metal railing that separated me from a fall of forty metres, I was perplexed as to why all other people seemed to approach these heights with the nonchalance of climbing a bunk-bed.

David with Sigiriya in the background (Evan is in the backpack)

At the bottom of the hill, we walked to the main town and drank the milk from coconuts, and coke. I wanted the water from the coconut to quench my thirst but to me it tasted like warm aspirin. The black western stuff was much more refreshing.

In the afternoon, we rested and swam as the clouds thickened. We lay floating in the water and watched eagles soar and glide on the hot winds and Rueben took his first doggy paddle.

Mary, Evan and Rueben went back to our room just before supper, as the first heavy drops tumbled out of the sky. The adult in me instinctively wanted to follow them when I saw my t-shirt getting wet. Carrie, however, was more reluctant and wanted to enjoy swimming as the droplets bounced off the pool water.

"Come on Dad, stay with me," she pleaded.

I paused and had to fight the urge to stop my t-shirt getting soaked.

"Come on Dad, when is the next time we can swim in a rain storm?" Carrie called out.

I was so glad that she cajoled me into staying with her. Sitting at the bottom of the pool and listening to plops of water the size of marbles hit the surface was lovely. I wondered if this is what it would be like swimming in a glass of Schwepps.

@@@@@

Carrie was my first-born and she made Mary and I wrongly believe that we were model parents. After Carrie was born, we attended many new parent events. On most occasions, groups of ten proud parents weighed down with an army of prams and bags full of baby sustaining equipment turned up for a barbecue on a beach in North Sydney (where we lived at the time). There were always one or two crying babies and parents with dark eyes trying to shut them up; wishing it was someone else's small baby making all the noise. By the time the barbecues ended, though, nearly all the children joined in the crying. If pain was a noise, then ten screaming babies would be close to an axe attack. Carrie, however, never joined in. She lay or sat looking around her, sucking her two fingers and watching the world around her, and Mary and I smugly thought it was our parenting that made her this way.

As she grew up, her desire to watch everything in the world gradually turned into a desire to be involved in everything in the world. I spent hours taxiing her around between trumpet classes, swimming teams, gymnastics, drama and junior wind band (where a collection of other like-minded small people gathered together and created a sound like a traffic jam). She gave most of these activities up eventually, but she wanted to experience all these things and see what they were like.

It was Carrie who wanted to swim in monsoon rains because she wanted to see what it was like. Now when I complain about a rainy day, Carrie always says that rainy days are the best. I often wonder if this is because of those monsoonal swims in Sri Lanka.

Chapter 4: Polonnaruwa

The next day we headed north-east for an hour. Unlike the ride to Dambulla caves, the journey to Polonnaruwa was on a luxury bus with a garish Buddha on the dashboard and gold stripes sandwiched into the brown veneer walls.

Having just had a visit from the Easter Bunny, Evan's mind was on chocolate as we found our seats on the bus.

"Dad is this what it would be like travelling inside an Easter egg?" he asked.

"No Evan, it's like the inside of a hollow poo!" Rueben shouted.

I could tell where his mind was focussed.

On the journey, I tried to focus my attention on the lakes and jungle outside, but my eyes kept returning to a film blaring from a drop-down screen in the aisle. The star of the film was a man with bucked teeth that were the shape and size of guitar plectrums. Passengers rocked with laughter as he tried to seduce a woman washing clothes in a creek. In the next scene, the man with the fangs stole a bike. When we got off at Polonnowura, he was wandering around a field in a skirt. I was so distracted, entertained and repulsed all at once that I cannot remember much else of the bus trip. I do remember, however, that I had the joyless job of waking Rueben after he fell asleep, curled up next to me like a hibernating field mouse, though Rueben was also hot and wet.

Polonnoruwa was built by King Parakrambahu. The greatest legacy of this king was the vast lake that he built near his city. I did not realise it at the time, but the road

36

our bus with the easter egg/hollow poo interior travelled along skirted the lake's northern edge. However, his ruined city is what most tourists come to Polonnoruwa to see.

This king was a devout Buddhist whose kingdom was weakened by Indian attacks and so to address this weakness, he urged the people to unite under Buddhism and embarked on a process of reforming the faith. True to his word, he fired sixty thousand monks who were only in the job for the money and kept the dedicated ones to serve the people. History looks kindly on the king and this is understandable; his desire to ensure that no drop of water was wasted led him to build a lake that is still used nine hundred years later to supply water for paddy cultivation in the centre of Sri Lanka.

The bus driver did us a favour and dumped us outside the tuk-tuk stop. At first, however, I wanted to shout at him for dumping us into a situation where a financial transaction needed to be negotiated. My feet had not even touched the tarmac before the approach.

"My name is Wiki and I am forty-six years old," he stated with a heavy accent.

It is odd what people tell you when they first meet. I remember I introduced myself to my current boss by saying that I lived in the same town as David Beckham and then told him about my intention to plant fruit trees in my garden. For me, I blurt things out when I am nervous and perhaps it was the same with Wiki.

Before we arrived, I had no intention of hiring a tuk-tuk. I imagined happily walking around the ancient city with the children as content with using their legs as they would be in playing on their game consoles. However, the wall of heat that knocked us as we got off the air-conditioned bus changed my intentions. Wiki wanted to charge us three thousand rupees, but I agreed on two thousand. In the blazing heat, I would have paid four thousand for the luxury. There was no way any of us could have coped walking through the ancient ruins of Polonnaruwa as it was hotter, stickier and more uncomfortable than a fat man in leather pants in the tropics.

Wiki may have been nervous, but he was a smiling and happy man with a lot of love to give. He drove us around in a pea green tuk-tuk with 'Wellcome all of you' painted on the roof and 'I love you more than my life' painted on a sunshade by the driver's seat. The breeze created by the movement of the vehicle provided some cooling relief and there was part of me that would have been happy to drive around the site a few times and then go and sit in a cafe. However, we were there to see old buildings and so we drove for a few minutes, jumped out of the tuk-tuk, looked at the carcass of a building or a pile of old bricks, jumped back in, went to the next set of ruins and repeated the whole process again.

Getting the children out the first time to look at a pile of old rocks was reasonable. However, after the third stop, places like the 'Royal Palace Bathing Pool' did not excite them and they got up from their chairs with the enthusiasm of a child who is told they would spend the next two hours washing up dishes. By the fifth stop, Rueben refused to walk and so I carried him around after that point. Wiki laughed at Rueben's stubbornness, and Rueben responded by scowling at our driver and folding his arms.

As many of the ruins were ancient Buddhist temples or stupas, we needed to remove our shoes and hats out of respect. Walking on stone that had baked in the sun for six hours was a painful experience. Having done it very briefly to look at an enormous round stupa that reminded me of a Kaiser helmet, the boys refused to burn their feet to look at any more ruins. I was therefore forced to carry both Rueben and Evan for a dash around the circular Vatodage; arguably one of the most famous of Polonnoruwa's buildings that once housed the Buddha's tooth. I think I ended up in a German's photo as I sped down the stone steps with Evan in my arms, grimacing as if someone was sticking nails in my back.

Wiki's tuk-tuk of love

My favourite place in the city was The Lankatilaka. It was an ancient Buddhist temple with twenty-metre high pillars and high walls that drew in my gaze to the bottom, where the remains of an ancient Buddha stood. Best of all, there were no signs asking me to remove my shoes until we got very close to the Buddha. The temple was immortalised by Duran Duran in the video for the song 'Save a Prayer'. When we were there though there were no Duranies (Duran Duran fans who travel the world to step in the places where Duran Duran once stood), and we shared the place with only a friendly gardener and a tribe of relaxing grey monkeys. Watching the monkeys whilst we rested in the shade kept us all entertained.

Evan asked me, "Dad, why do monkeys have eyebrows?"

It was a good question. One I had not considered before.

Evan sitting in front of a stupa at Polonnoruwa

Back in the town we ate curries and drank coke. Carrie and Evan had pancakes and Rueben had a roti that he spat out like the pith from a combine harvester. We purchased onion bread fried in the shape of a doughnut and ate jalebi. It was all delicious.

"Dad, I need the toilet!" Evan looked at me in alarm.

We had to climb up a flight of stairs and go past rooms with double mattresses on the floor, all unmade. I wondered if the place was a brothel.

"Dad, why are there so many unmade beds here?" Evan asked, peering into one of the rooms as we hunted for the lavatory.

"Ah, I think this is a place where friends have lots of sleepovers," I responded.

Evan seemed happy with my answer, and stood in silence as he relieved himself, and I was thankful that he was distracted onto other things.

Wiki was outside when we finished our late lunch. He waved us over. "If you want a seat then go to the bus station."

The cynic in Mary did not trust what he said but we took his offer up. By the time we passed the bus stop where we would have embarked had we not taken Wiki's advice, the bus was full. Wiki was a good man. However, the great things of the day kept coming. Just as I fell asleep on the bus journey home, a local shook me.

"Elephant!" he stated as he pointed outside to the banks of the ancient man-made lake, with a smile on his face.

Chapter 5: Minnerya National Park and Ritigala

The following day, we decided to take a walk through the village of Digampathana, to the main road and the largest shop in the village. The children pleaded with Mary and I not to walk due to the heat and the dogs, but we stood firm and assured them that walking was good for their souls. We started the journey, though the children walked in silence with their heads and shoulders down. Evan stomped to show his displeasure. I led the way with the children following behind. As we came to the edge of the town, a middle-aged man and a woman on a moped slowed down as they approached us. I heard them laughing and chatting behind us as they crawled to a walking pace. The moped came to a stop next to me.

The man asked, "Where are you from?"

"England", I said breathlessly.

Having just got the children to use their legs, I was not in the mood to stop and chat.

"Where are you going?" he asked.

"Just up the road to the shops," I responded.

I stopped walking because it would be churlish, bordering on rude, to continue.

He spoke with his wife in a quick staccato and joyful tongue, there was no command or anger. She smiled, laughed and disembarked.

"I ride you," he insisted and pointed to the back.

"But the kids, I'd like them to have a walk."

"They ride as well," he responded. "Come," he said to the children and patted the saddle.

Immediately Evan and Carrie jumped on without looking at their parents. It was clear that any opportunity that involved avoiding walking and dogs was to be taken with great joy and haste by them. I had no choice.

Wearing no helmets, Evan, Carrie and I firmly gripped a stranger around the waist as we drove up past the waiting dogs. They barked at us, but this time the canines had no chance to cause any damage. Carrie and Evan laughed at them, knowing their malevolence was in vain for now. Riding a motorbike for the first time and avoiding a walk and the dogs left the children very happy.

"This is so cool Dad!" Carrie exclaimed.

"Just make sure you are gripping hard!" I retorted.

I was not certain if our insurance would cover head injuries of children riding mopeds with no helmets. On the main road and outside the shop, the tuk-tuk drivers sat up when they saw us getting off a moped and spoke at the friendly man. I think they were concerned about the cost his kindness had on their business, but the friendly man waved them away and insisted we were his friends. Carrie and Evan went into the shop ahead of me to choose some treats and I followed behind.

After we made our purchases, our new friend insisted he take us back to where Mary, Rueben and the man's wife stood at the front gate of the resort. When we arrived back, we exchanged pleasantries and thanked them, and they insisted that if we have time, we should visit them. They told me where they lived, but it was in broken English and I politely listened but could not understand the directions. As they left, we all waved them off.

Even Rueben waved enthusiastically. Whilst he was peeved at missing the moped ride, he was also glad not to walk or encounter dogs. As he waved, he must have taken a few steps back. The first thing I knew something was wrong was when I heard a splash, followed by silence, followed by a scream. I turned around instantly and ran towards Rueben. The reception staff dived across to assist me.

My youngest son fell into a small pond. It only took a few moments to get him out, but my heart was thumping with the fear that he was badly hurt. A few moments of anxiety passed as we made sure that there was no physical damage done to my son, but everyone quickly saw that the only damage caused was to some juvenile fish. We all laughed except Rueben, who continued to wail as if he had just had an enema inserted into his back passage. As I led him past the dining hall the cooks and kitchen staff came out, laughed and tried to high-five my young son. He looked sternly beyond them and refused to interact as water dripped from his nose.

"No need for a swim then Rueben!" I said as I tried to improve his mood.

"I wanted to swim in the pool, not the pond!" he shouted at me.

Clearly my mood improvement strategy was not working and so I tried distraction.

"Guess what Mum has gone and done?" I asked him.

"What?" he asked.

This strategy was working.

"She made me book us a tour to see some elephants!" I responded, trying to sound joyful but I probably sounded sarcastic to a trained ear. Fortunately, Rueben was too young to detect mild derision.

I did not want to go on any tours, particularly tours that included seeing wildlife since there were no guarantees that the wild animals would make an appearance. A few days before, in Sigiriya, Mary saw an advertisement at a local tourist office for a jeep safari to see wild elephants. I pleaded with Mary, but her insistence was stronger. Carrie was also very excited about the opportunity to see these creatures and so I knew the battle was lost. Ten minutes later, I paid several thousand rupees for the trip and arranged a pick up by jeep.

"I want to see elephants Dad," Rueben replied.

The storm had passed.

Once Rueben was calmed after his pond dip, and after we all had a pleasant siesta, we waited in the car park at the resort for twenty minutes with no sign of the jeep. The heat of the day still fizzed in the air and left us drenched and sticky. Mary insisted that the jeep would come, but I was less confident. Our resort was fifteen kilometres away from where we booked the tour and it would be easy for them to take the money and deliver nothing. After thirty minutes of waiting, I telephoned the number on the receipt. They were hesitant at first, and I heard frantic gabbling in the background. It was apparent that they forgot about us.

"Yes, David Tucker, jeep comes."

The phone went dead.

Finally, a jeep arrived. The driver looked about sixteen years old.

"What tour you on? Elephant?" he asked, smiling.

I was not certain that he even knew where to take us.

Jeeps in Sri Lanka are more like trucks, with metal benches in the back with a frame to hold a canvas sheet to protect the passengers from the elements. Even though it was late afternoon and cloudy, he insisted that he transport us with the back entirely closed. We raced along the roads to the Minneriya National Park and had to shout to communicate with each other over the roar of the engine that echoed under the covers. There would have been a wind from the movement of the vehicle, but as we were sealed up in the canvas that went over the frame, we slowly cooked like a baked potato. When we finally arrived at the entrance to the national park and the sides lifted, we all gulped for air.

The driver smiled at us.

"Fun, yes?" he asked.

Mary and I had an acute sense of irritation with the driver, who promptly disappeared into a Rangers hut and came out with a cup of tea.

Once fully refreshed, the driver came over, "you need to pay fee."

"What?" Mary and I responded in unison.

"You need to pay fee," he stated again, smiling.

"But I was told that all costs were included in the tour."

"What?" Mary whined as she looked at me.

"We need to pay a fee," I said, assuming Mary was whining at me.

"I know, I can hear the man speaking as well," she retorted.

I shook my head and held my jaw tight. "I'll just pay. Not much else I can do is there?"

I did not tell Mary that I paid another forty dollars for the entrance. I made a mistake of telling her how much I paid for us to climb Sigiriya, and her reaction was ugly. Sometimes it is easier to keep quiet.

An hour before sunset, we joined a convoy and entered the park. A man dressed in khaki and a hat that made him look like a guard from Jurassic Park sat with us and gave a rehearsed speech about the park.

"Will he want a fee as well?" I thought, smarting at his presence and feeling irritated that I was right in my reluctance to even take this tour.

By now, I felt so ill-humoured that I could not remember anything he said, but I noticed that his moustache looked like it had fallen from his nose, for there was a visible gap between the nares and the bristly hair above his lip.

We drove along a winding dirt path with overhanging trees and thick jungle foliage. Occasionally we stopped to what our guide claimed was wildlife, though all I ever saw was a shaking branch. I stood and stared resolutely ahead. Suddenly, we drove out of the jungle and onto a vast grassland that went down to a lake. I remember the guide telling me that when the monsoon comes, all the grassland we drove on would be submerged in the lake waters. The sun sat low on the horizon and we parked up. There were no elephants. I wanted to say 'I told you so' to Mary but knew that comments like that would simply be like throwing a match on gunpowder.

We sat in silence and the children complained about feeling a bit hungry.

"Look, look, look, look!" the guide said excitedly as he pointed over at the wall of foliage of the jungle about a kilometre away.

I saw nothing at first in the trees, but my eyes were not trained to spot wildlife. However, a few minutes later, I saw what the guide saw. A herd of Indian elephants, at least twenty, appeared from the jungle and slowly walked towards us. I instantly entered a beautiful state of ecstasy at the sight. All that ill will I felt towards the tour and my wife fell from me. It took them well over thirty minutes to walk from the protection of the jungle to us; grazing in the long grass as they walked. Monkeys scarpered in front of them, foraging in the sunset. It was a beautiful and idyllic scene. Finally, the elephants were within twenty metres of the vehicles.

By this time, Evan and Carrie sat with their heads in their hands, complained of hunger and told us many times over that they were bored. Rueben, Mary and I remained in rapture at these wild creatures passing so close to us. I had such awe for these animals that I wanted to embrace and hug as many people as I could and there are reams of photographs with me embracing the family. Even the irritating driver and our guide with the fallen moustache would have received a cuddle had they come close to me.

All the guides in the convoy requested silence as the elephants walked by the vehicles. It was surreal to hear the heavy thud of their feet and the ripping of the grass as they grazed. Suddenly Rueben could not contain himself and burst into the chorus of "Jesus love is very wonderful!" He sang as loudly as he could, much to the amusement of our guide and a troop of stunning young Scandinavian women in the vehicle behind us.

The elephants at Minnerya National Park

I watched the elephants' pendulous rear ends lit up by a setting sun with monkeys playing around them as our driver started the engine and turned the car around.

"Dad I'm absolutely starving," Evan whined with his head cupped in his hands.

"OK Evan. We'll go back now," I responded dutifully. I did not want to leave.

The tour was an amazing experience. Sometimes

even my wife knows best.

After the safari, we asked our young driver to drop us in the town of Habarana, several miles from the hotel. We ate delicious curries in a restaurant with orange and green walls that made it look like a set from a children's television show. American wrestling blasted from a television suspended from the ceiling; strangely at odds with the décor. No one spoke as we ate, mostly because we were so hungry, but partly because we were tired and partly because the children were transfixed by the men in tights jumping on each other.

The family with the elephants at Minnerya National Park

By the time we finished, it was dark and the only lights on the busy road were the headlights of the tuk-tuks and cars. In the darkness and being the solitary tourists, the town felt a little sinister. All of us wanted to take private transport back to Digampathana so that we could rest. However, being tourists, all the drivers quoted us a price that was more appropriate to riding the few kilometres back in a rocket ship. We went up a line of waiting drivers and even resorted to waving others down, but their price fixing was solid. I was irritated and was about to admit defeat.

"Can I help?" a man asked.

I wanted to tell him to get lost, just like I wanted to tell all the tuk-tuk drivers. However, I remained calm and told him our predicament. He walked off and I thought that was going to be the last I saw of the stranger. We stood and resigned ourselves to getting a bus and running the gauntlet of the dogs of Digampathana. However, to our surprise, out of the darkness, our stranger arrived with a driver in a tuk-tuk who gave us a fair price. I shook the stranger's hand and warmly thanked him for his help. He smiled shyly and walked away into the night.

As we drove into the night, our driver introduced himself as Hashan. He told me that he saved up for three years to buy his tuk-tuk and then he handed me his business card and asked if there was anywhere we wanted to go the following day then we should call him.

@@@@@

The following morning, I called Hashan to take us to Ritigala. He was a bit late in arriving and Rueben was hot and fractious. Hashan walked over to Rueben, smiled, picked him up and placed him in the driver's seat, which left Rueben stunned and oddly compliant.

"I have a younger brother," he said proudly.

"I'm his Dad and I wish I had that effect on him." I responded with a smile.

Ritigala is an old Buddhist monastery in the jungle on the side of a mountain. Unlike Pollonoruwa or Sigiriya, Ritigala is on a rutted dirt road and was not quite on the tourist map compared to the other ruins. To get there, we drove through Habarana and over a bridge. Suddenly Hashan broke and went down a dirt path by a bridge.

"Look, look elephant!" he shouted.

It was great to see the locals get so excited about elephants that seemed as common here as squirrels are in England. I have never taken a taxi in England and had the driver pull over for me to look at a squirrel before, but here it seemed common for the locals to get excited by the local fauna. He pulled over. We scrambled down the litter-strewn banks to see a captive elephant soaking in poo green waters. It looked catatonically happy to be having a soak and seemed about as interested in us as it would be in a leaf. Still, being in its presence left us all smiling, though I think we were all happy to get back on the rickshaw and get moving to feel a breeze in the infernal heat.

At Ritigala, the children were not interested in the ruins, but the insects; Christmas beetles with blue dots that looked like pretend eyes, tiny blood red beetles and butterflies with wings the size of a baby's hands. As we walked up a brick path that led up the mountain, monkeys jumped through the trees, though we heard only the rustling canopy and saw the shadows as they passed above us. The path meandered up through the jungle and past circular platforms and stone bases that Hashan said were temples. Trees towered above us with buttress roots that gave the trunks the same shape as soviet rocket ships.

The only piece of antiquity that the children liked was a decorative urinal stone. It was the prettiest bit of carved masonry that we saw in Ritigala. The Buddhist sect that lived in the monastery at Ritigala were simple folk who lived in austerity. They even walked around in the shrouds that they lifted off dead people. To splash into these intricate urinals was a reminder to the monks of their decision to live austere lives and as a sign of their ambivalence towards the more regular breeds of monk. Evan and Rueben were disappointed they could not give the stone a road test.

That evening, we took a walk from the resort for the final time. Instead of walking into Digampathana, we turned the other way and walked towards the great rock of Sigiriya. Unlike other nights, the storm clouds did not roll in and the wind seemed perfectly still. The sun sat low on the horizon and the sting of the heat of the day had gone.

We walked five hundred meters down the red dirt track when one of the happiest men I ever saw called us over. The man was on the cusp of looking old, but he did not let any age show in his movements. He moved like a man who had just married his first love. His house was a shack made from corrugated iron with bricks on the roof to hold it down, and great piles of tree stumps at the back for cooking fires. The house sat at the front of a field the size of a football pitch. Beyond that, the wild scrub in the sunset turned the colour of fire and looked incredibly lush.

We spoke no Sinhalese and he spoke very little English, but he introduced us to his wife who also beamed as if on a quiz show. Both insisted that we toured their farm. They showed us their neat rows of beans and squash. All the children were amazed at the beans growing out of the dusty ground and crouched down as the man tenderly stroked the immature stalks and spoke in a language that they did not understand.

As we were about to leave, he called us over to his well that was the size and depth of a swimming pool. We spent another thirty minutes peering over the edge of a great well looking at fish and an ancient turtle who they named John. The wife plaited wild flowers in Carrie's hair inbetween running across the fields to scare off the wild peacocks.

The very friendly farmer and his wife plaiting flowers in Carrie's hair

We never knew the names of these kind people who showed us their home and life, and welcomed us like long lost relatives, but their kindness was one of the most beautiful moments that I experienced in Sri Lanka.

Our final swim that night ended abruptly as the sky lit up and the pool attendant in the white shorts rushed over and told us to get out as he feared we would be hit by lightning on his watch. It was probably best, as we had no time to get sad about leaving a place where we spent so many hours.

Walking back to the resort after our time with the farmer.

Chapter 6: Unawatuna and Galle

We were booked to stay in Unawatuna just south of Galle; our hotel was a collection of cabanas crammed onto a small plot of land. Our cabana was the furthest away from the reception and, to get to it, we walked through a verdant garden full of shrubs with leaves the shape of badminton racquets and plants with pink flowers. Tiny black and white birds darted around the branches, and chameleons sat; frozen, hoping not to be noticed. Our cabana was vast and full of chocolate-brown wardrobes and enormous coffee tables. Frilly net curtains hung across every window and in the largest room, there was a four-poster bed. If someone was to film the story of Heidi and move the setting from the mountainous Alps to the tropics of Sri Lanka, then the cabana would make the perfect set. We all sat on the bed and looked around us; half in confused awe, half in mild disgust. It felt a little like we had the cabana where they stored all the old furniture and was only used in emergencies. As I looked around, I realised that the place had no chairs.

"We would never have been given a room like this in Sigiriya," Carrie said.

She was right.

After seven hours in a taxi, we were dirty, and Carrie wanted to wash her hair. The shower looked like a brown telephone box with a myriad of buttons and nozzles. It was called the 'Delux Steam system' and had the look of an appliance that would fire powerful jets of water at the user. Carrie was very excited at the prospect of this, but despite much pressing of buttons, she could only make it play the radio.

That evening, we walked down the road towards

the main village of Unawatuna. It was the first time we saw the sea in Sri Lanka and we chose a restaurant with tables that were placed on the sand where we could soak up the atmosphere. The children were very excited about the menu because burgers and chips were on offer, rather than rice and curry. It should have been idyllic, but the portions were small and twice the price compared to Sigiriya. I looked over at the other guests at the restaurant and realised they spoke with a Yorkshire accent and were sunburnt. In the darkness there was nothing to make us feel like we were in Sri Lanka. It felt more like the Costa Brava. We returned home poorer and forced to fill up on biscuits. No one was willing to admit it, but we regretted leaving Digampathana to come to the coast.

The next morning, we ate breakfast and returned to the beach in the hope that a new day would improve our thoughts about the place. The walk left us sweltering. Rueben was adamant that he would only proceed if he sat on my shoulders, and the Sri Lankan women all waved at him as we passed by. They thought he looked very cute wearing his 'floaties', though his sweaty thighs felt like warm sponges dipped in mild acid on my cheeks and left me with red sweat marks where they rubbed.

The previous evening, it was too dark to take in the view. However, in the daylight, we looked out over the lovely curved bay for the first time. The bay ended in a small headland with a stupa and a golden Buddha in a shelter facing out to sea. Jungle foliage came down to the sea edge and hid the conurbation, and banana shaped fishing boats painted the same sky blue as the colours of Manchester City football club sat beached in the sand. The fishermen added stabilizers to the boats by lashing together coconut tree trunks and driftwood. As it was still early, we had the place to ourselves.

"Yeah this is definitely pretty," I thought.

For the first time in Unawatuna, I felt pleased to be

there. In the morning light, the place looked stunning. I chased the children into the choppy seas and spent an hour playing in the turquoise waters. Carrie dove for shells and Evan spooned mud into his swimming trunks. After a swim, Rueben fell asleep in the shade of one of the fishing boats, lying with his arms splayed out like he was shot. After a swim, the rest of us waited for him to wake up; squinting as the sunshine reflected on the yellow sand.

By late morning, the sun was high enough to burn our skin. With this risk in mind, I woke Rueben and we returned to the hotel. However, the walk back after that first swim was hard work. Evan cried in pain from chaffed thighs due to the large amounts of sand he shoved down his trunks, and Rueben fell asleep again on my shoulders and so whenever I walked, we banged heads. His hands fell over my face and the sweat from his palms stung my eyes.

Rueben asleep in the shadow of the boat at Unawatuna

Whilst I was eager to get back, Mary was eager to avoid a repeat of last night's poor culinary experience. She noticed an anonymous house that advertised local Sri Lankan homemade food if we gave a few hours' notice. So, she knocked on the door and explained to the owner that we were a family of five and that we ate everything except the youngest, who only tolerated bread. I kept on having to jerk my head to move Rueben's hands and see what was happening. As Mary turned away, I was certain the owner looked back at her with a look of confusion mixed with alarm that suggested he did not understand what she said.

In the evening, there were fireflies in the bushes and frogs on the pavements as we sprinted to dinner in a monsoonal shower that was lit up by fantastic electric pulses. To avoid the rains, we picked a moment when the showers slowed and ran to the anonymous house. We made it half way before the monsoon shower picked up again and so we were soaked when we arrived, but it did not matter. It was quite refreshing. We sat in a makeshift shelter in the front yard of a family house behind a picket fence made from driftwood. Whilst we waited for our dinner, we played a game of chance based on the colour of the tuk-tuks that passed by, and then we ate beautiful curries as the rain pelted against a corrugated tin roof.

@@@@@

The following day was a public holiday – the Sinhalese New Year. The holiday seemed very important to Sri Lankans as almost every shop was closed. It reminded me of Christmas Day in the UK. On Christmas Day, I have my rituals that include watching the children open presents at hours usually experienced by milkmen and breakfast television presenters, followed by sprout

58

peeling and then church. Sri Lankans begin their special day by cleaning the house, lighting the lamps and then visiting their families. Each ritual is marked by an activity that usually involves loud noises.

With little to do, we ate a breakfast of fruit, omelette and toast and then swam in the curvy pool at the hotel. Suddenly, just after ten o'clock in the morning, the whole town erupted in loud firecrackers that made us instinctively duck for cover. They produced a lot of smoke and made the air smell like a battlefield. Later, on the way to the beach, we passed the small temple on the main road and there were very happy families banging drums. The Sinhalese New Year is not a day when you want to have a headache.

The beach was packed with joyful day-tripping Sri Lankans from nearby Galle. Compared to the previous day, this was rush-hour. The ladies wore their saris and paddled in the waves; keeping a watchful eye on their children. The men wallowed in marginally more nudity in groups further out to sea, but never far from the shoreline. Everyone appeared to be happy and talking together.

My children played a game that involved sitting in the path of a breaking wave and taking the full force of its energy in the face and up the nose. They nearly always rose up out of the water gasping for breath and coughing. To me it looked a little like torture, but they assured me it was fun. I sat by our beach bag and casually created a dome in the sand. Mary rested next to me and I too was tempted to close my eyes, but knew the water was too dangerous for small children to risk a catnap.

Close by the children, two young men stood and looked at me before talking between themselves. They reminded me of teenage girls talking about a boy they saw and liked at a disco. Suddenly they turned and walked towards me.

"Excuse me Sire, but are you England?"

"I am from England and I speak English. No one has ever called me Sire before!" I responded with a wide smile.

They smiled back and looked like they did not comprehend what I just said.

"May we sit with you and practice our England?"

"Of course, I'd be honoured to talk with you."

My eyes felt heavy and I had little desire to get the mental gears going for conversation. However, with their company, at least I would not doze accidently. They sat down next to me. The silence that followed felt pregnant with awkwardness and even though they approached me, it was clearly me who needed to lead the conversation. I had no inspiration about what to ask them.

"So," I paused, trying to think of a question. "Why are you at Unawatuna?" I asked.

They told me they were at the beach for a holiday but lived in Galle. One of them was looking for work and the other was a therapist. They tried to explain to me the significance of the fireworks in the morning and said something about Buddha and Sinhalese, but their English was not good enough and I did not understand. Despite this, the conversation flowed reasonably easily but only if I kept the language to a basic level. We covered areas like their favourite subject at school, how many brothers and sisters they had, how old they were, if they were married, their favourite food and their favourite cricket player. When I asked about food, their faces lit up and they invited me to their house to eat; seemingly not realising that I was here with my family.

After thirty minutes Mary awoke, and the men became surprisingly unsure about continuing the conversation. They glanced over at her as if she was a matron about to come at them with a large syringe. With little warning they made their excuses, shook my hand

and carried on walking down the beach.

The clouds thickened and with the threat of sunburn reduced and nothing better to do, we played for several more hours at the beach; building sandcastles and having races into the water. As the temperatures cooled in the late afternoon, we strolled along the beach to a large headland with a Buddhist statue sitting proudly at the end.

Just as we were about to turn off the beach and head up the hill, Evan stopped at a sign, spent a few moments reading it and then called me over.

He turned around to me and asked, "Dad, who is electric bill?"

I was a bit confused until I joined him at the sign. It said, 'Please donate to electric bill.'

"Is that the name of the statue on the hill up there?" Evan asked as he pointed up at the Buddha.

It was my afternoon to deal with innocent people, and it was beautiful.

@@@@@

Evan is my middle child. He celebrated his birth by defecating inside the womb and so his first moments outside were spent lying on a resuscitation table whilst an army of doctors checked his lungs for poo. However, a prodigious bellow that sounded a little like his voice had just broken assured doctors that there were no turds in his airways.

If Carrie lulled us into thinking we were fantastic parents, Evan excelled in making us realise that we were just like everyone else. His deep throated cries sounded like he smoked and permanently had croup, and he cried as if the night would never end. When he had his afternoon sleep, he woke in such a foul temper that only an hour of children's television and an astonishing amount of food could calm him. Trying to get him to sleep of an evening was my job and often required multiple visits and a huge dose of patience. I think those early days with Evan were the most tiring I ever experienced.

Having said that, he became a toddler and mellowed into a gentle boy with a great love of slapstick comedy. He spent hours watching 'Tom and Jerry' cartoons and roared with laughter with a gusto like Brian Blessed. Above all, though, Evan loved reading and left piles of half-read books next to the toilets around the house. His reading gave him a genuine interest in the world and his favourite card game involved identifying countries based on flags; a game he nearly always won. His reading also made him question a lot and sometimes he asked questions that were hard to answer, such as "Dad, why am I here?" and "Dad, why do I need to go to school?"

It was his questioning mind that made him ask, "Dad, who is electric bill?"

@@@@@

The first Portuguese who landed in Sri Lanka got there by accident. He went by the name of Dom Lourenco de Almeida and, had it not been for a storm that washed him ashore near Galle, then it is possible that this city may just be an anonymous headland today. Dom Lourenco obviously took quite a shine to the place because within a year he built a factory to process the valuable cinnamon that grew like weeds in Sri Lanka and negotiated deals with the local king. Over the next one hundred and fifty years, the Portuguese developed the area and built a fort at Galle as a coastal defence. However, in 1640, the Dutch came along and took a fancy to the Portuguese endeavours, and, after a brief siege, they stormed Galle and carried on where the Portuguese left off. The Dutch made much of the fort and high walls that exist today.

For me though, Galle was not about forts, but cricket. Mary and I lived in Sydney for seven years and rented the back half of a house that was owned by an elderly couple named Malc and Jan. Malc was a sound engineer for the Australian Broadcasting Corporation but retired long before we met him. He spent all the money we paid in rent on sailing and travelling around the world, visiting the great cricket stadiums. He knew Lords, the Oval, SCG, MCG, WACA and Eden Gardens. However, the one stadium of the world he always wanted to visit but never got to was Galle.

I remember in 2006 speaking with Malc after the Boxing Day tsunami. We spoke about the devastation and he spoke particularly about his sadness at the destruction of the cricket ground in Galle. There were so many pictures of the devastation caused by the Tsunami. For me, however, the photo of the scorched earth of the cricket ground and the buses that were thrown around the pitch was the one I particularly remember. If it was not for my conversation with Malc then I think Galle would just be a place on the tourist map for me.

Just before we left Australia to return to England, Malc knocked on the door wearing an enormous bandage on his scalp that looked like a skullcap. He explained to me that the skin doctor found a melanoma that was so aggressive and deep that the cancer was likely to be in his skull. We returned to England and not long after, we received the news that Malc had died.

In 2007, England went on a tour of Sri Lanka and they played at Galle just before Christmas. It took just over a year to repair the ground and England were the first international team to visit. It was a poignant moment in cricket and was a milestone on the road to recovery for Sri Lanka. For me though, I remember listening to the test on the radio and thinking about Malc, and the test ground he never saw.

@@@@@

The bus dropped us outside the cricket ground. Unlike the pictures I saw of the test cricket, when I visited it was locked up and lifeless, like a kiosk at the seaside in the middle of a British winter. I spent a few moments looking at it, but the children were hot and did not understand my interest in the place. They wanted to get to some shade and get away from the buses whose engines spewed out hot air and smoke like a hair dryer close to death, and so we moved.

It was a public holiday again and almost no shops were open. Even if they were open, we could do little business with them since we were running low on cash and no banks were open. We wandered past the locked gates of the Dutch reformed church with a façade that looked like a decorative tombstone. Like the cricket ground, the place looked packed up and the only sign of life was an enormous lizard the length of two shoeboxes sunning itself on the steps. The sun left us soaked in perspiration. The only cool place we found between the Dutch reformed church and the lighthouse at the end of the fort was a very expensive tourist shop that sold paintings and lacquered Sinhalese masks. Prices in the shop were so high, only wealthy sportsmen and idiots would consider a purchase. I guessed the owners needed to fund their air conditioning by some means. We spent no money in the shop but did spend several cool minutes admiring shiny carved wood and smirking as we thought about the stupidity of people who would consider paying the shop's quoted price.

We reached the lighthouse at the end of the fort. Underneath the lighthouse, the locals swam at a small beach and lounged under a Banyan tree. Evan and I looked down longingly at the swimmers enjoying the calm and turquoise seas; wishing that we had our swimwear to enjoy a cooling bathe in the inferno. Reluctantly, we turned our back on the beach and wandered down streets flanked with houses with deep wooden verandas. A group of Japanese tourists were the only people walking those streets with us. They too seemed equally as sweaty and nonplussed that all the forts shops and historical buildings were shut for the public holiday. Desperate for respite from sunshine, we lounged in the shade of Banyan trees by the courthouse and watched local boys play cricket; smashing a tennis ball into the far corners of the square and diving around on hard bitumen. Evan and Carrie enjoyed watching the game and we were all thankful for the breeze that licked comfortingly at our foreheads and armpits. Rueben was content chasing a cat with as much flesh as a pencil into an enormous storm drain.

The road into the fort at Galle

We walked out of the fort and to the train station to find out the times of trains to Weligama. At the station we purchased some delicious green grapes from one of the few open shops and ate rice and curry in a filthy restaurant. Carrie looked at us and pleaded, begging us not to eat in such a place. However, she devoured an egg roti and after that, the sweat and grime ceased to matter.

On the bus back, we drove to the outskirts of Galle, I looked back at the fort, and the cricket ground before the vista was blocked by a ship with a rusted and punched-up hull. I glanced up at the people on the bus and the concrete buildings that lined the wide harbour and wondered what it must have been like when the tsunami waves broke land on Boxing Day in 2006. Looking around I could see no evidence of what happened, but I guessed there must be scars.

Chapter 7: Weligama and Taprobane Island

The following day we waited at Galle train station for the slow train to Weligama. We moved to the middle of the platform to sit on some blue plastic chairs at the station. It was so humid that we all grimaced at the effort of just getting to the station from the hotel. The day had barely begun.

"Mum I feel like I'm slowly rotting." Carrie said.

The chairs looked new but when I sat on one, I was immediately tipped back as the base came away from the legs. I stood up, embarrassed at my heavy-handed vandalism. We all moved several metres away from the broken chairs to distance ourselves from the damage and hopefully blend into the small crowd waiting on the platform with us. Rueben and Evan, however, seemed bent on making us the focus of attention and fought like little puppies. They needed constant separating. I looked over at the crowd. All the locals stood with their arms folded and stared at us. They did not sweat, nor did they break the seats, nor did their children hit each other.

In the heat, Mary turned on the boys. "If you two don't stop mucking around then one of the locals here might tell a policeman and have you arrested!"

The fear of spending the rest of their youth at the mercy of the Sri Lankan judicial system made them stand still with their heads bowed, as if they were waiting to see a headmaster. I looked at Mary who suddenly realised that her warning had not only had the effect of stopping the raucous play but also paralysed them with fear. She immediately softened her stance.

"Boys I am so sorry, the police are definitely not

67

going to arrest you for playing," she pleaded and gave them a cuddle.

So much for consistent messages to children.

The train arrived and so we embarked. However, the moment we took our seats, all the lights and fans turned off and a nice cool environment inside the carriage quickly morphed into a sauna. Our legs stuck to the tired leather chairs and standing up gave us all the unpleasant sensation of a gentle waxing on the underside of our thighs. It left us irritable and grumpy. I was about to get off and make sure we were on the right train when suddenly the sky-blue fans on the ceiling whirred into action and we started to move. Soon after, we had a sea breeze blowing through the carriage and the journey became delightful as we trundled through jungle.

Rueben made friends with a little girl; they smiled at each other and played 'peek a boo' even though they spoke no common words. As the train picked up pace, both squinted as they looked ahead into the breeze that pressed their soft hair flat against their foreheads.

At Weligama we walked through urban chaos that seemed to shimmer in the damp heat.

"Hello Sir! Where you going? Hello, where you from?"

Tuk-tuk drivers waved us over and parked their vehicles to make it difficult for us to pass. The whole atmosphere felt oppressive and left me barking unfairly at the children to move past the crowd as quickly as possible.

The main practical purpose of the visit was to go to the Bank of Ceylon to change money. With the banks shut over the Buddhist New Year, the queues snaked out of the building when we arrived. It looked like I would wait for hours. Mary and the children sat in the shade of a tree against a wall and I approached the queue and joined the back. Almost immediately, a security guard approached me and pushed me to the front. Within five minutes I was handed over one hundred thousand rupees in return for my US dollars. It came in a wad of cash that was almost an inch thick and was impossible to place into wallets. Mary and I had no choice but to store the bundle in our day packs. For the rest of the day, I constantly looked at everyone around me as a potential thief.

Weligama was noisy and hot. We wanted to escape but had no idea where the beach was and so had no choice but to take a tuk-tuk to the coast. I think the drivers could smell the money because they quoted a fortune to take us the few blocks. Perhaps they were used to Westerners paying a lot of money because very close by was an island that had been patronised by rock stars and presidents for a century.

@@@@@

Taprobane Island would have been an anonymous place where the locals took their cobras had it not been for Maurice Talvande, but this man took a snake infested rock and arguably put Weligama on the map. Maurice was a showman, raconteur, playboy, liar, artist, gardener and visionary. In his early days he changed his name to the more aristocratic sounding Count de Maunay Talvand and travelled around England and America giving lectures about living in a French chateau; a surprising thing to have an insight into since his Dad was a humble local banker in the town of Le Mans in France. The count was a social climber and through the lecture circuit, he connected with the rich, the famous, the royals and the 'hangers-on' like himself.

It was in this new social status that he met Mary Byng. Mary was a lady who had a close relationship with Queen Victoria in her youth and had a dad with a title, and that meant that she too had a modicum of blue blood pulsing in her veins. She had a strong personality and decided to marry Maurice to spite her father who did not approve of the man. Ironically, Mary and her father fell out previously because Mary did not approve of her father's choice of lover – Cara Colgate a widower whose husband made his money from toothpaste.

Maurice and Mary married and decided to run a boarding school in the Loire valley for rich boys who wanted to polish up on French. It seemed a perfect set up with Maurice's showman antics and command of French and Mary's useful network of wealthy families. All started well but soon clouds of scandal enveloped the married couple. Many of the young men accused the count of waking them at night with unwanted sexual requests. The property owner of the chateau heard of the allegations and insisted the school be closed, and the couple moved back to England.

In England, the couple lived on opportunism and lies. The Count got credit by telling people that he would soon inherit a small fortune from his dying mother, and Mary sold her story of her friendship with Queen Victoria to a newspaper. Maurice's mother eventually died but the inheritance was small and within a year the count declared himself bankrupt.

World War One took a terrible toll on many people and families, including Maurice Telvande. Having experienced and witnessed war and its associated horrors, he yearned for a place where he could escape, where the world seemed perfect. His search finally ended on a visit to Ceylon where he rounded a headland and saw an island that the locals named Golduwa or Rock Island, just offshore in Weligama bay. In the Count's typical manner, he took it upon himself to rename the island Taprobane – the original Greek name for Sri Lanka.

His first job was to get rid of the cobras. The locals used the island as a dumping ground for the snakes. Once they were evicted, he made himself a house with uninterrupted views of the sea and planted a perfect garden with trees and foliage so verdant that it looked like they were exploding off the island. Despite his scandals, lies and bankruptcy, Maurice Talvande appeared to take his sorrow and channel it into this island to create something beautiful.

Once he died, the place became a hotel for the rich and famous.

@@@@@

We disembarked a few hundred metres beyond Taprobane Island. Litter and broken coconuts spoilt the scrubby grass at the edge of beach, but the aspect of the island covered in trees was a lovely vista. We wandered barefoot along the beach. I noticed we were the only international tourists around, but there were plenty of locals. Some were involved in a game of cricket that involved stumps made up of a few tropical fronds propped up by coconuts. We sat in shade that we shared with a thin cow who appeared to have unhelpfully pooed in all corners untouched by the sun.

The sea between the island and us was too shallow for anything except wallowing and so we took a tuk-tuk to Mirissa, a few miles around the bay. At Mirissa, the sea was rough, and people surfed the waves. Mary suggested that we find another area to swim, but I had other ideas. As a compromise to show that the sea was safe for us, I took Carrie (the strongest swimmer of the children) into the water. Almost immediately, a wave smashed into her and left her face down in the yellow sand.

"I told you it was too dangerous." Mary chided me as she cleared out sand granules from Carrie's nostrils. Based on the evidence, this was an argument that I was not going to win.

We walked half way around the bay. Rueben announced earlier that day that he would not walk in the sunshine, and, true to his word, I had to carry him on my shoulders. In the soft sands of Mirissa beach, I sank above my ankles with each step and it made my groin strangely ache. We were desperate to cool off in the late morning heat. In the distance, I saw a group of Sri Lankans in the water and standing on the shore; a sign that indicated safe waters. On a paradise beach that was over a kilometre long, there appeared to be just twenty metres of calm swimming waters and that was in the in the lee of a small island.

The family and the walk to Taprobane Island

I swam with the children and locals in this lee. As we bobbed up and down, we saw several turtles with their heads poking out of the water. Carrie is a fantastic swimmer, but knowingly sharing her water with anything larger than an animal the size of her hand left her nervous, and she decided that this sea was not for her. As she was leaving, one of the locals shouted and looked like he was straining. Carrie turned and ran out of the water; frightened by the man's whoop. I thought he caught his foot under a rock and needed help, but to my surprise he lifted a turtle with a shell the size of a large dinner plate out of the water. He hoisted it above his head and hollered in excitement. In his triumphant pose, he strangely reminded me of a female Wimbledon champion holding their dish aloft for the photo-call at the end of the final.

Boats on Mirissa beach

Locals gathered around the man and his captured turtle, took selfies and even placed sunglasses on it. The turtle moved its head from side to side and moved its flippers wildly. This disturbing sight captivated the children. It was difficult to make a choice between causing a fuss and addressing the stress that the local were undoubtedly causing the reptile. I was about to go and plead with the locals to let it go when, fortunately, they also decided upon this option themselves.

After the turtle incident, none of the children wanted to go into the waters.

"Come on Carrie, swim with me, turtles aren't dangerous," I said.

"Yeah Dad, but what about the animals that eat the turtles?" Carrie responded.

Walking along Mirissa beach

Her fear fuelled the boys' fear. Our swim was over. Within a few moments of leaving the beach, the sun left me damp with sweat and made my eyes sting. The sand was so soft that it was hard work to walk on it, and Rueben held firm in his policy of refusing to walk in the sunshine unless under extreme duress. It was easier to carry him rather than fight him. We walked over to the main road to get a bus back to Weligama and stood by a bus stop. There was no shade and we had no idea of the

74

bus schedule. To make matters worse, the sun's heat reflected off the asphalt road and a breezeblock building next to the road blocked any cooling sea breeze.

Without warning a large gate creaked open and an old woman with an enormous but toothless smile beckoned the children and Mary into a house to wait in the shade. She spoke no English and we spoke no Sinhalese. However, she was effective in guiding the family in with a few hand gestures. She was also effective in using her hand gestures to tell me that I should stand outside and keep an eye out for the bus. Whilst I stood outside, Mary later told me that the children sat next to a fan and ate fudge whilst the woman showed Mary a faded doily with a picture of Queen Elizabeth in the 1970s printed on it.

"Bus!" I shouted urgently and waved my hands, dancing in the same way as Jeewana did a few days previously.

I had no desire to remain in the heat on that roadside for another thirty minutes whilst my family ate fudge in the cool shade and ushered them out of the house as if it was on fire. I was not going to let this bus pass. We sped away from the kind woman's house and never said a proper goodbye, but we did say thank you repeatedly in English, much to her amusement. The more we said it, the more she seemed to laugh. In the violent breeze caused by the movement of the bus racing along the coastline of Weligama Bay and with the view out to Taprobane Island, the world seemed beautiful.

Back at Weligama we were hungry and tired, and so found ourselves a place to eat curries and rice washed down with a cold and refreshing coke. Rueben suddenly crossed his legs and looked at me in alarm. He had so much focus on playing with his weapons (a pile of used and crushed straws) that he forgot about the sensation to urinate.

"Ah toilet?" I asked the restaurant owner.

"No toilet," he replied, but confusingly pointed down a corridor.

There was a small wet patch on Rueben's shorts as we tore down the corridor. I opened a few doors but saw only dark and oil-stained cupboards. There was no time to reconfirm my understanding with the owner. Rueben and I burst into a brightly lit yard. I was still running with him as I whipped down his shorts and he instantly let forth a powerful jet that washed a significant portion of dust off a bush.

"There, that's clean now," he remarked as he wandered back inside and down the corridor. Job done.

"Mum, I cleaned a bush!" He said as he grabbed his straws.

Almost as soon as we sat down an old man wanted to say 'hello' to Rueben. Initially Rueben was reticent to engage, but when Carrie and Evan agreed to go with him, he went to sit with the old man and allowed Mary and I to eat in peace. He chatted in broken English and even gave the children some chocolate.

As we left, Carrie spotted hundreds of bottle tops littering the pavement and gutter outside. She started picking them up and put them in her hat. The shop proprietor leant over the counter and looked amused and confused in equal measure. He opened the door and beckoned her inside to pick up the bottle tops from around the counter. She left with a doggy bag full of bottle tops, but to her it was treasure. To this day, she still has her collection of bottle tops, though now they are a little rusty with age.

The bus back to Unawatuna was packed. Rueben slept all the way, curled up in the foetal position in the lap of a plump Sri Lankan mother. She smiled and cuddled him, and his presence appeared to make her day. Carrie sat between two old men on a chair and Evan fell asleep and rested his head on a young man, much to the amusement of the young man's travelling friend. The sun sat low as we rattled along the coast road back to Unawatuna. In the bush between the sea and the road were hundreds of gravestones, a permanent reminder of the tragedies that have beset Sri Lanka over the last few decades.

As the bus sped along the coast road with an engine that sounded like an angry tractor, I thought about the old man in the café, the old woman at the bus stop and the shop keeper giving Carrie his bottle tops. I looked over at my children spread around the bus; resting against or cuddling locals. It occurred to me that the great thing about the day was not the sights or the beach, but the kindness of strangers.

Chapter 8: The Hospital and Galle

On our final day in Sri Lanka I woke up unable to move my neck, and the inside of my ear felt like it had been rubbed by sandpaper for several hours. My glands felt swollen and even though I felt like I would look like the elephant man, a casual look in the mirror ensured I still looked disappointingly normal. Mary had to squint to see any swelling, but she could tell I was in some discomfort. There was no way I would be happy without painkillers. It felt like an ear infection, and so I decided to go to a doctor. The receptionist directed me to a tuk-tuk and wrote down the name of the private hospital in Galle.

The hospital was one of the finest I had ever visited. It was clean, modern and very well run with reception staff dressed in blue saris and incredibly well-presented. The nurses who attended to me before the doctor turned up were obviously not expecting a six-foot white man waiting for them and instantly giggled; holding their hands to their lips as if telling a coarse joke. I too giggled but for different reasons. The young women still had white nurse's hats, pinafores and spotless white socks and shoes. Their uniforms did not look like they had evolved much since British rule, but it was the happiness on their faces that made me forget for a few moments about the pain. This was most certainly not the National Health Service in the UK. They stood to the side with their shoes together and their arms folded looking at me.

Thirty seconds later, a doctor entered. He was a small and young man. Immediately the demeanour of the nurses changed. They stopped laughing whilst the doctor examined me. The doctor was so small that, to look inside my ear, he needed to get me to slouch in the chair.

"Well that's something new," I replied and smiled as I shuffled down.

I never thought a doctor would instruct me to slouch in a chair. As soon as I spoke, I saw the nurses biting their lips trying to supress hysterics.

The doctor gave me a prescription and left.

"Goodbye," I said to the nurses.

They smiled and waved farewell. As soon as they left my presence, I heard them walking down the corridor behind the examination room howling with laughter. I turned the prescription into drugs at the local hospital pharmacy and was back eating breakfast at the hotel within an hour of leaving. Looking back, I do not recall a more pleasurable medical examination than the one I had in Galle private hospital and would recommend it for anyone with a minor ailment. Judging by my experience, you will make the nurses happy with your presence.

That morning we relaxed by the pool. Carrie, Evan and Rueben befriended a family from Huddersfield and they spent most of the time in a make-believe Olympics where they dived, swam and belly flopped. They all had Greek names; Carrie was Apollo, Evan was Poseidon and Rueben in his floaties took the title of Zeus.

As the day ended, we took a tuk-tuk to Galle. It was the final evening. We stood by the lighthouse and ate chilli-infused samosas that we purchased from a man on a bicycle. Mary took a photograph of us all sitting on the edge of the wall eating them. Looking at the photograph months after it was taken, Evan was wincing as if he had just rubbed his knuckles against a cheese-grater. To calm the pain of the chillies, we found another man selling pieces of cut mango. The evening sun shone through the black clouds and turned everything the colour of rust as we walked along the fort walls. A breeze blew up off the sea and for the first time in Sri Lanka, I did not sweat, nor did I feel like I was walking around in a used nappy. After a few minutes looking out on a vista of the Indian Ocean and the tin rooves of Galle fort, we came to an open grassed area; a natural amphitheatre where there were several games of cricket being played. Some of the older groups had cricket bats but others used a splintered fence panel and a tennis ball.

A cricket game in Galle with Rueben and Carrie

We sat and ate the mangos and watched the cricket. A child holding a piece of wood returned to his mum. His mum pointed at us and smiled. At first, the young boy was nervous but after some motherly cajoling, he approached us cautiously, dropped the bat at Carrie's feet and ran back to safety. The mother then pulled out a tennis ball from her bag and threw it over at Carrie. For the next half hour, Carrie played cricket with her younger brothers, with Rueben having the most time with the bat.

Suddenly the storm broke. It started with the occasional plop of heavy rain but judging by the activity of people quickly packing away food and possessions, they knew what was to come. Evan grabbed the tennis ball and ran to give it back to the mother, but she smiled and waved him away as he approached with the ball.

"A present," she responded.

We raced to the buildings and tried to take shelter in the lee of a house but were quickly ushered into the building (it turned out to be a guesthouse) and to the sheltered roof where we watched the streets of Galle fill with water. The storm blew in and then disappeared quickly. Within five minutes, the cricketers took to the field again and we took that as a cue to continue our walk. We thanked the people who beckoned us in and continued along the walls towards the clock tower, but this time there was a rainbow over the terracotta and tin rooftops.

The nocturnal insects were in full voice when we ate in a restaurant by the bus station. Just before we left Galle, we purchased some delicious sweets from a vendor. Rueben burst into hysterical laughter as a toothless peanut seller with bulbous eyes snuck up on him like a tiger and tried to steal the tennis ball. Mary and I.looked on, surprised that he was laughing rather than crying; for the man had almost no teeth and his eyes looked like they were about to pop out of their sockets. For a five-year-old, we thought this would have been the stuff of nightmares, but it appeared we were wrong, and his laughter drew a small crowd of vendors and tired-looking workers.

@@@@@

It was over. That evening we had a few hours' sleep and then took a taxi to Colombo International Airport and boarded a flight back to London. Mary insisted that the children try to sleep but Evan was in no mood. His mind was filled by questions, "Which airline is better,

Qantas or Emirates?", "Are there more countries in the Southern Hemisphere or the Northern Hemisphere?", "Where do Kuwait Airlines pilots do their shopping?" and then finally, "Dad, how far is the airport from the ferry station that could take us to India?"

My eyes burnt from tiredness when we arrived at the airport. I felt more exhausted than when we arrived two weeks before, but I knew such fatigue was transient. As the plane took off and we strained to see the early morning light on the groves of coconut and the beach below, Evan turned to me.

"Dad has Sri Lanka ever been in the World Cup?"

"The football one? No, I don't think so," I responded.

"If they do then they will be my second favourite team", Evan stated after a pause.

I knew what he meant.

Rueben and Carrie by the clocktower in Galle

Chapter 9: After our return

Just after we arrived back, we relayed our adventures to Mary's parents. Her mother turned around and asked, "How could you visit a country like that with their terrible human rights abuses?"

Mary's mother referred to the civil war between the Tamil Tigers and the Sri Lankan military. The civil war lasted over twenty years and an estimated one hundred thousand people were killed.

It was a fair question and one that I considered before we went and whilst we travelled in Sri Lanka. The problem with asking that question is that I had no tools available to answer it. To be honest, I had so many amazing experiences there it was easy to bury this uncomfortable issue in the haze of travelling memories.

After some internet searching, I discovered a book called "This Divided Island" by Samanth Subramanian. The author met and documented some of the characters involved in the civil war and I found the book helpful in understanding this tragic chapter in Sri Lankan history.

I read the book on the train whilst travelling into work in London and came across an account of the Kattankudy mosque massacre. On the 3rd August 1990, the Tamil Tigers disguised themselves as Muslims to avoid suspicion and then went to three mosques in the town. At the point where the locals knelt for prayer in the mosque, the attackers pulled out grenades and automatic rifles. By the time the Tamil Tigers finished firing, one hundred and forty people ranging from the ages of six to seventy-eight years old were dead. Of all the people in the mosque, there were only three survivors.

In the book, one of the survivors told the account

of the final moments of the youngest victim who was called Akram. After the initial spray of bullets in one of the mosques, the Tamil Tigers shouted out, "Everyone who isn't injured, get up and help us take the injured to hospital." At that point Akram jumped up and, in tears shouted, "I want to go home, I don't want to be here." One of the Tamil Tigers, walked over to him, put the gun in his mouth and pulled the trigger.

I suddenly realised Akram was Evan's age, and could read no more. I wept openly on the 0903 train much to the confusion of a bald man who sat opposite me, trying to answer some emails on his phone.

Should we have visited a country where terrible human rights abuses have been committed? As the train made its slow way into London Liverpool Street, I thought about the kind farmer and his wife in Digampathana who welcomed us into his home and plaited flowers into Carrie's hair. I thought about the married man who left his wife with Mary whilst he took the children and I up on his moped to the shops, the woman who fed my children fudge whilst I baked in the sun at the bus stop and the lady who was thrilled to hold Rueben as he slept on the bus.

Should we have visited a country where terrible human rights abuses have been committed? Emphatically yes. It suddenly dawned on me that Sri Lanka suffered through civil wars and a tsunami that, between them, took one hundred and thirty thousand souls. I failed to see how keeping away from the country would be an effective protest. Even if it was, it would probably add to the suffering of a country that to me seemed crammed full of decent and honest people who were genuinely interested in us and showed my family amazing kindness.

In a perfect world, this would have been the end of the chapter. However, on the morning of 21st April 2019, Islamic militants walked into three hotels and three churches in Colombo, Batticaloa and Negombo and killed two hundred and fifty-three people, many of them children. I found myself weeping once more for this senseless loss of life. As a Christian, this attack felt personal because people who share my faith were targeted and slaughtered. Heartbreakingly, it emerged a few days later that the terrorist cell that committed this atrocity was based in the same town that suffered so much in the massacre in 1990 – Kattankudy.

At the time of print, most Western governments advised against all but essential travel to Sri Lanka in the wake of these attacks. All travel warnings by governments should be adhered to, particularly when travelling with children. However, I still maintain that this country is crammed full of decent and honest people who showed my family amazing kindness. Tourism contributes around ten percent of total income to the country and so this government travel warning will hit the country hard – especially many of the people we met. I pray for this country, for the families who have lost and for the security situation to improve. Sri Lanka is a wonderful place, I personally hope to be back soon.

Vietnam

Hanoi

Ninh Binh

Holong Bay

Dong Hoi

Hue

Hoi An

Ho Chi Minh City

Ben Tre

Chapter 1: The Mekong and Ben Tre

On one side of us were houses; some of them had roosters kept in cages the shape of washing baskets on their front lawns. The birds crowed constantly as if reminding each other of their bravado and prowess in a fight. On the other side was the Mekong river bordered by shrub and mud banks. In the reeds on the river, soggy fake money floated in the still waters and plastic coke bottles sat marooned in the mud. Boats chugged along the brown waters; all of them had painted eyes on their hulls. I found out later that this was to help the boats see, and to scare away the crocodiles that occasionally escape from farms farther up the river. The boats sounded and looked exhausted, with cabins and shelters made from cracked weatherboard and covered in peeling paint; they reminded me of the kind of boats that Popeye lived on.

Sweat ran down our backs as we walked into town. We hoped for some respite from the humidity once we got to the centre of Ben Tre. Carrie walked next to me and I knew from her heavy footsteps and pained look on her face, as if she was suffering from a neuralgia, that she saw little point in this excursion.

Across the bridge and ahead of us, a large two-story building that covered an entire block stood on the riverfront and looked as familiar and functional as a council office built in the 1980s in the United Kingdom. Only the red flag of Vietnam flying from a pole at one corner suggested anything different. In the absence of anywhere else to go and desperate for some respite from the heat, we headed to this building that was shown on the map as the main town market.

"Dad how long are we going to be here for?" Carrie asked as soon as we entered.

For a young woman who was developing into a

prodigious shopper, this was a definite show of disapproval.

"Well let's just have a look around," I responded a little irritated. "We have no timetable."

We walked down organised rows of women wearing the traditional Non-La hats (cylindrical hats worn by the Vietnamese) with baskets of ducklings or chicks surrounding them, past rows of people standing amongst great piles of imitation brand jeans and sunglasses. Being in such an unfamiliar place, our nerves propelled us forward. We did not want to stop moving and quickly came to the edge of the market where there were rows of shallow pools full of fish waiting for their end.

Boat on the Mekong River

"Hey Dad, there are a lot of fish here. Do people have ponds in Vietnam?" Evan asked.

"I'm not sure these are sold as pets," I responded.

That second a vendor scooped up a fish, showed it

to the customer as if she were a haberdasher showing off a piece of lace, gained approval for the sale and then smashed the fish over the head with the handle of a knife. The customer and the fish vendor carried on talking as she sliced off the gills and fins and barely looked as she gutted and carved up the carcass that still quivered in shock.

"Oh, that is absolutely gross!" Carrie exclaimed, and impulsively leant back, sending her hat sailing into a shallow pool of fish.

Rueben stood, staring with his mouth open as he watched the butchering progress.

"What's that white thing I can see?" he asked pointing at the innards. "Is that a cushion inside the fish?"

Mary pulled at her son's hand, but he was reluctant to move. I retrieved Carrie's hat and apologised to the vendor, who smiled politely.

"Hey why don't we go over here? It looks like they're selling sweets," I said.

In the distance, I saw piles of what I thought was pink foil and thought I led everyone to the sweets section of the market. As soon as we entered that area, I realised that we walked from the fresh fish area and into the dried fish area and the pink reflection were the shiny glazed scales of dried fish. It smelt like a cavern full of hot vomit and blocked gutters.

"Rueben, it smells like your poo!" Evan declared with the typical mind of a boy.

Rueben laughed; proud that his older brother thought he could produce such powerful odours. Comments like that went one of two ways. Rueben either laughed at the toilet humour or took offence and moved in for a punch. In the heat and the unfamiliar environment, I was thankful he saw the funny side.

"Please can we get out?" Carrie pleaded.

Mary and I were now very happy to get into the

fresh air again. Feeling hot and tired, we sat and drank cokes by the river on chairs that were of a suitable size for a children's tea party. My knees came up to my chin. We sat and drank the familiar black liquid, and watched people haul sacks full of neat brown parcels that looked like bags of heroin off the weatherboard hulks. Our children cooled down and even smiled. Nearby, children played cards and we listened to Vietnamese spoken for the first time, and the world seemed happy again.

That afternoon, I kept falling asleep as I adjusted to the time difference between the UK and Vietnam. I did not want to risk falling asleep and then struggle to sleep at night, so I persuaded Carrie to come with me on a bike ride. We cycled through the countryside around Ben Tre, along quiet roads that cut through unfamiliar jungle foliage and past people cutting coconut trees where the recently cut wood was the colour of rust. We passed groves of grapefruit, hundreds of foraging chickens, graves made from cement and painted green, butterflies with huge wings and birds of paradise flowers that added colour and beauty to the piles of rubbish that swam or festered in the gutters. Suddenly the road fell into the muddy waters of a tributary of the Mekong. I did not want the journey to finish at the ferry crossing, but Carrie needed some cajoling to take a ferry across the tributary.

"Come on Carrie it will be fun. There are some beautiful wooden bridges on the island that we can cross."

"You are kidding, aren't you? We are going to an island to look at bridges?" she responded.

I realised that cycling to see wooden bridges in temperatures above thirty degrees was hardly a selling point to an eleven-year-old.

"Well I can't leave you here, so you'll have to come," I responded.

If the carrot did not work, then I instinctively resorted to the stick.

90

Carrie glanced over at the ferry.

"I'm not sure that looks safe," she said.

"Clever girl," I thought.

She knew her mother would not approve of a boat that looked like a large motorised tray traversing a fast-flowing river and subtly pointed that out.

"Don't worry about Mum. By the time she knows we will be back safe with her, in which case it will be too late for her to do anything except tell me off. The worst case is that the ferry will sink and we will drown, and then she will blame me and not you, but neither of us will care since we will be dead."

"I don't want to die," Carrie said without a pause.

"You won't," I responded quickly, and then added, "Trust me. I'm your Dad."

I sat down in the scant shelter on the ferry. The driver sat above us on an elevated platform and so I had a perfect view of his mosquito-bitten ankles. He chatted away to all passengers in Vietnamese and then steered the boat with his feet rather than his hands. A middle-aged woman wearing a Non-La, who looked like she only knew how to smile, sat next to Carrie and caressed my daughter's cheek. She kept repeating something in Vietnamese that I did not understand. I was nervous, and so was Carrie.

"You marry me, yes?" she asked me with a delighted twinkle in her eye. I realised she was missing most of her front teeth.

The ferryman looked down at the scene below, said something and then laughed. Carrie looked at me and bit her lip; unable to do anything to control the situation and a little frightened by the toothless woman.

"Sorry," I whispered. It was my desire to see wooden bridges that led us to this situation, and I felt guilty. "Are you OK?" I gently leant into her.

Whilst the ferry was uncomfortable, the island that

we cycled along was lovely, with car-free roads the width of a coffee table and views over citrus groves and coconut trees. The ride was a pleasure. Even Carrie warmed to her enforced adventure.

"So, what's so special about these bridges anyway Dad?" she asked.

"They're not special really. They're wooden. The photos I have seen make them look like they have been taken from a film set of Robinson Crusoe," I responded. "They look really photogen-."

Suddenly about thirty metres ahead of us we saw a gang of enthusiastic guard dogs prick their ears up.

"This doesn't look good," I thought.

Carrie cycling on the island just before we encountered angry dogs

We stopped pedalling as the canines eyeballed us. One of them sat up. It looked at us for a moment and then bared his teeth. At this point, I failed at being the protective Dad. The ferry across the Mekong was an acceptable risk to take, but being ripped apart by a pack of dogs was not high on my list of possible ways to die that day.

"Turn around!" I shouted at Carrie (who was ahead of me and therefore closer to the dogs). To my shame, I did not wait to ensure she was following.

"Dad, wait!" I heard Carrie call from behind me, half panicked and half laughing as she pedalled trying to keep up with me.

We never did see the wooden bridges.

That evening we ate a delicious Vietnamese soup called Banh Canh. It contained broth, noodles and slices of chicken and pork. Evan tried using his chopsticks the wrong way and a stern and motherly worker in the restaurant walked over to him, scowled, took the chopsticks away and force-fed him. Rueben refused to sit on a stool, so Mary and I took turns holding him so that each of us could eat in peace. Carrie ended up casually picking up a chilli and was about to place it in her mouth when the same lady that force-fed Evan ran over and pulled it out of Carrie's hand like she was a baby armed with a sharp knife. In embarrassment, Carrie rubbed her eyes and face, and then had to walk back to the hotel with her eyes streaming due to the chilli.

As we crossed the bridge and walked to our hotel, Evan laughed, "At least you didn't rub your balls!"

Carrie looked cross.

"I don't have balls," she responded curtly.

I felt sorry for my eldest daughter; through her actions, her hat smelt of fish, her dad forced her onto a ferry that she did not want to go on, he left her to a pack of baying dogs, her brother teased her about her anatomical differences and now tears fell from her face due to a firm chilli-rubbing.

@@@@@

Seeing life on the Mekong is difficult without going on a tour, and the following day we took a tour with a young guide named Kim. She had long straight hair and always smiled, but Carrie at the age of ten was still taller than her. What Kim lacked in height, she made up for in enthusiasm and energy, and as soon as she saw us, she went to work on our names.

"What is your name?" Kim asked.

"David."

"What is your name?"

"Carrie"

"What is your name?"

"Mary."

"What is your name?"

"Evan"

"What is your name?"

"Gary"

I have no idea why Rueben decided to call himself Gary that day. Perhaps it was in deference to our minister at church with that name.

"And my name is Kim!" She said as she spun around as if she was showing us her new dress.

"I like you Kim. You seem happy." Rueben said, and then he turned around and continued eating his breakfast.

"Thank you!" Kim said, "I like you too." She clasped her hands together and laughed at my youngest son's honesty.

Minutes after our introductions, we crossed the road, hopped onto a boat and joined the flow of vessels chugging down the river. As soon as we passed the town, thick impenetrable jungle hung over both shorelines with an occasional hut or tin roof interrupting the tree line.

Our first stop was a brick factory. Whilst interesting

to see how the bricks were made, the visit was an uncomfortable ten minutes. When we arrived, the workers glanced up at us with filthy and exhausted faces but did not show any interest in our presence, and carried on working. They made bricks out of the Mekong mud and used rice husks to fire the bricks in beehive-shaped kilns. There was a single machine to shape the bricks. The rest was sweat and hard work.

Ten minutes farther down the river, we stopped at a coconut processing factory. It was an enormous shed made from corrugated iron, with the husks of coconuts rising in piles ten feet high. Under the shelter, the husk was separated from the nut and the nut was emptied of the oil and the white flesh. All the bits were used to make decorative bowls, mats, oil, soap and coconut wine. Even though the work was hard, the people here laughed and chatted when we arrived (though mostly about us rather than with us). One of them, who spoke a little English, asked if they could buy the children, much to Carrie's embarrassment.

The sweet smell of coconuts filled the air and walking around the floor was like walking around on a spongy brown mattress. Even though we were in the shade, sweat poured off our bodies and the humidity made me feel spent, chaffed and itchy. I felt soft and a little ashamed as I climbed aboard the boat. There was no way I could work in that kind of environment like those nut crackers and factory workers.

We cruised up a narrow tributary where the foliage crowded in around us and formed a tunnel. The dark brown trunks and the waxy green leaves of the water coconuts created an impenetrable wall of greenery.

"Women and children hid in this plant to escape US helicopter guns. People born after the war had no noses due to Agent Orange." Kim said.

Agent Orange was a herbicide that the Americans

sprayed over Vietnam during the war. The herbicide removed the jungle foliage and so, by spraying it, the US hoped to deprive the enemy of food and concealment in the jungles. It is estimated that three million people across Vietnam have suffered sickness from Agent Orange including cancer, birth defects and stillbirths.

She paused. "People say better to be taken by crocodile than die by US bullet."

I knew the area around Ben Tre suffered terribly in the Vietnam War. In 1968, the North Vietnamese army infiltrated deep into South Vietnam and US strongholds and attacked their enemy over the Vietnamese Tet holidays. Ben Tre was a town in the middle of the offensive and levelled by the consequent fightback by the US forces. A colonel, shortly after the levelling of the town and contributing to the death of over one thousand civilians, reported to a press officer that it was necessary to level the town to save it. In other words, it was better that the town and its people be destroyed than fall into Communist hands. His comments were published around the world and did nothing to arrest the decline in support for the US presence in Vietnam.

The jungle began to close in and soon the river was just wide enough for the boat. We slowed and eventually came to a stop next to a cosy shack that looked more like a café from Gilligan's Island.

"Welcome to the coconut candy factory!" Kim told us with an enthusiasm that is rarely seen outside couples announcing an upcoming pregnancy.

We saw vats of boiling sweet-smelling coconuts and sugar, and the cutting up of the long slabs of toffee into small rectangular chunks that were wrapped up and sold as coconut sweets. However, the thing that really grabbed the children's attention was something that the proprietors would not allow us to see. As soon as we arrived, they covered up a large cabinet with a decorative turquoise cloth. It was as if they were about to do some magic.

"What's in there?" Rueben asked.

Kim asked the workers, who responded in Vietnamese.

"There is a big snake. She is eating now."

"What is she eating?" Evan asked

Again, Kim asked.

"Chicken," Kim responded.

"Please let me see!" Rueben asked.

The workers refused to pull back the sheet despite my children's pleas.

As soon as the children's attention was diverted by a hot vat of cooking sugar and coconut, I peeked behind the curtain. I saw a ball of feathers squeezed by an enormous constrictor. Two chicken legs stuck out of the curled-up snake and kicked in the bird's final death throes.

Out of respect for the owners, I had to pretend I did not see what I saw. We sat at a table and ate fruit that had white flesh with tiny black seeds that looked like poppy seeds. From behind the curtain, I heard a crack of bones.

"What is this fruit called Kim?" I asked.

"That fruit is dragon fruit," she responded

I knew the fruit's name, but I wanted to disguise the bone-cracking noises.

Many fruits in Vietnam look like testicles and our guidebook accurately described the dragon fruit as looking like sore testicles, but they tasted delicious. I told Rueben this fact in the hope that such associations would make them more attractive to his taste buds, but he just scowled when I offered him a taste. I also noticed Mary scowling. However, her scowl was more at my unorthodox approach to make fruit more appealing to a young boy. Knowing I would likely be lectured a little later, I sat in silence and drank lime and honey tea, ate bananas the size of a cigar and longan berries with pips that looked like eyeballs.

After our fruit snack, we left the river and took a tuk-tuk to an unknown place in the jungle and wandered down a path to a wooden shelter. We sat at a ramshackle table and under a roof made from palms, where we drank coke and ate a delicious fish that came displayed on a toast rack with its scales peeling off. It looked like it had been through a nuclear incident. The fish was called 'Elephant Ear'; hardly surprising considering its' pancake shape. We ate the fish by tearing off the flesh and wrapping it up in rice paper with cucumber and pineapple. Then we dipped it in tamarind sauce and shoved the delicious food into our mouths. Rueben thought it all disgusting, which surprised me because I thought tearing flesh off animals to eat appealed to a small boy. Afterwards, we lay in hammocks shaded by thick jungle and deflated gently as the food digested.

Our final part of the tour on the Mekong was on a wooden canoe down a small river where the water coconut trees created a low natural arch. Kim made us all wear Non-La hats for the journey. I felt stupid, as if I was on a tour in France and made to wear a beret but went along with it to avoid looking churlish. She was such a joyful person that it was difficult to decline anyway.

@@@@

Our stop in Ben Tre should have been a respite after the long journey from the UK, but I awoke the following day at three-thirty in the morning full of cold, covered in sweat and feeling a lot worse than I did when I first arrived in Vietnam. We were all up at that time intentionally to take a taxi back to Ho Chi Minh City airport with the hope that everyone slept in the taxi. However, the taxi driver insisted on travelling with the air-conditioner on full. He made the car so cold that he had to use his wipers to get rid of the condensation and we all shivered rather than slept, though I shivered mostly because of a mild fever.

At the airport, the woman at the check-in smiled at us as if we were the best thing to have happened to her so far that day. She was very personable, and her joy made me feel a little special as she took her time, carefully studied each passport and pressed her buttons to print out the tickets.

"Thank you, Tucker David and have a nice day". I was not sure why she swapped around my surname and first name, but it did not matter. I smiled back, though I felt weak and wanted to sit down. Next, we joined a queue to get through security and, as I habitually did, I counted each passport. Four.

"I must be tired," I thought and counted again.

Four. I was a passport short. I checked the bags. Nothing. My heart pounded.

"Mary, are you holding onto a passport?" I asked as if she had stolen the last biscuit.

"No, of course I'm not! Passports are your area!"

"Yeah I'm missing one."

"What do you mean? It must be there!" Mary snapped at me.

As soon as Rueben and Evan join queues, they usually start fighting. This was no different.

"Stand still!" I barked, more to release some panicked tension than because they should not be playing.

I turned and ran back downstairs to the ticket desk. I felt like I wanted to vomit. The check-in woman was with someone else and had the same careful focus and serene smile she had with us. It took an age for her to finish with the customer. I jumped the queue, possibly ignoring all protocols.

"Ah, passport missing?" I asked.

She looked at her desk and fumbled with some papers. It was not there. The smile that made me feel special now seemed a little thin. She searched through another pile of papers. Not there. She moved her chair to make sure it was not on the floor. Not there. I had visions of spending the next few weeks in Ho Chi Minh City pleading with consulate officials. Under the final pile of papers, she felt something, dug deeper and out fell my passport.

"I am very sorry, Tucker David!" There was a pause between each word as she handed over my document.

My heart still pounded from the incident minutes later.

We cleared security with a guard who was more interested in talking with Rueben than checking our passports, so a loss may not have mattered too much anyway. If it was not for Rueben's presence, then I think we would have been an anonymous family.

The stress of a misplaced passport coupled with the early morning start began to rub off on us all. As we ordered drinks at the expensive café, Evan mumbled as he gave his order.

"For goodness sake Evan, speak clearly!" Mary blew up in her usual volcanic way.

Evan burst into tears. I glanced over at the Vietnamese waiters as Mary snapped, and noticed they stared at us curiously, like we were mating bears in a zoo.

Chapter 2: Hoi An

At Hue airport, we took a taxi organised by our hotel in Hoi An.

"So, first stop is a beautiful view of a beach and then the American bunker and then Marble Mountain", our young driver said. The syllable 'tan' on the word 'mountain' was emphasised, as if it was a command.

As we left the carpark at Hue airport, the children fell into a deep sleep and looked as interested in seeing sights as they would be in rifling through bins.

"I am pleased to take you on tour," he continued; smiling at me as he looked through the mirror.

Our driver clearly did not take a hint from the sleeping children. I felt freezing in the air-conditioned car but sweated with a fever.

The first stop after an hour was to look at a vista of a modern bridge and the Vietnamese coastline. We stopped on the edge of the road. Even though I felt like I had drunk a bottle of whisky the night before, I felt compelled out of respect for our driver to get out and see the view since no one in the family except Rueben was interested.

I grabbed my camera, got out of the car, helped Rueben out and walked a few metres down the road. I then lined up a shot and depressed the shutter.

"Dad. "

I ignored my son and squinted in the heat; wishing my head would stop pounding.

"What's this railway line down here?" Rueben asked.

"I'm not sure Rueben. Where is the railway line?" I responded as I lined up another shot.

"Down this cliff," he responded simply.

I turned around immediately. My son had managed to squeeze through a crack in concrete railings designed to allow rain water to flow off the road. He stood on the edge of a fifteen-metre-high precipice with the Hanoi to Ho Chi Minh railway line directly below. Not wanting to alarm him but realising his danger, I ran up and grabbed him and pulled him up over the barrier to safety. I looked over at the car and sighed in relief; thankful that Mary did not witness her son's near-death experience and her husband's negligence.

"Nice view," I said as I climbed back in the car.

"Why are you panting?" Mary asked as I closed the door.

"Must be my cold," I lied.

@@@@@

We stopped next at some concrete bunkers made by the Americans during the war. I am certain they were historic, but the number of tourists and associated infrastructure to see three old concrete bunkers bewildered me.

Our guide cynically dropped us outside a café and as soon as the car door opened, I was welcomed by a chubby Vietnamese man with a gold chain.

"Hello friend, cold drink? Beer? Coca cola? Iced coffee?"

"No thanks. We hope to be here for only a few minutes," I stated.

"When you get back then."

The salesman responded with such arrogance that Mary and I made a pact; only if we went into anaphylactic shock from touching a 1960s American bunker would we do business with the man.

Even as I write this, I am confused as to why so

many people found a few American bunkers on a hill so interesting. There was even a bride regaled in her wedding dress having her photo taken next to a crumbling concrete wall. By the time we arrived, it was midday and the heat was unbearable. We climbed dusty paths up to the bunkers that were covered in unknown animal crap and wildflowers. At the first bunker, Rueben wanted to rest in the shade, but Mary insisted we walk since the place stank of urine. Evan and I pressed on up the hill. He managed to fall over in the only area that was flat and had no rocks. Carrie saw one bunker and then returned to the road and sat on a rocky ledge looking sweaty and miserable; desperate to escape the strange place.

She looked how we all felt.

The single kind thing I can say about the place was that all the shops had signs outside that advertised 'Dung Maps'. At least having shops with the name 'dung' in it left the boys laughing as we drove away.

Our final stop on this tour that the family did not want to take was Marble Mountain. Marble Mountain was a limestone outcrop full of caves and Buddhist shrines on the outskirts of the coastal city of Danang. At the foot of the place were shops selling marble statues that would be perfect on the set of 'Dallas'.

"You interested in my statue? Come! Look! We ship!"

I was too tired to respond.

"We need to climb the stairs to see the caves," I told the children.

"What? Dad that's stupid, look there's a lift," Carrie groaned.

"It's good for your health to climb stairs."

I felt too worn out to add any spin to soften this requirement and I was in no mood to part with money to pay for a luxury such as a lift.

Carrie and Evan looked like they were going to

burst into tears as they faced the stairs. Rueben did not care since he knew I would probably carry him.

"So, what is here then?" Mary asked.

She knew exactly what was here. It was her way of asking if the climb was worth the effort. I looked at the children and sighed; knowing that if I lost Mary at this point then even seeing the caves (the solitary thing that interested me on the stupid tour) was at risk. With this in the forefront of my mind, I purchased tickets to use a lift that was awkwardly stuck onto the side of a hill in a vista that reminded me of 'Thunderbirds'.

There was one cave that I wanted to see where the sun broke through the roof and lit up the altar. Unfortunately, there were fifteen caves to visit and I was uncertain which cave was the one I wanted to see.

"You are not intending we look in every cave. Are you?" Mary stated.

Inside the cave in Marble Mountain

She had an amazing knack of making questions sound like statements when she needed to. Fortunately, the second cave we entered was the cave I wanted to see. It was stunning. Sunbeams shone through a small hole in the roof and illuminated the cave beautifully. I could have been in the opening scenes of 'Raiders of the Lost Ark' and wanted to spend much longer poking around in there.

"Come on!" Mary barked.

I could see that soon she would side with the children.

A potential mutiny on Marble Mountain

We left the cave and decided to buy a coke as a reward for everyone and to keep tempers calm, but two unexpected things happened. First, as we approached a vendor to make the purchase, the vendor appeared to be picking nits out of the hair of her friend and this put us off the purchase. Then, we passed a person just as they took a photo of a Buddha set in a pagoda and then turned to walk backwards. This was a sign of great disrespect and a guard in a khaki uniform shouted at the tourist, who was so shocked that they looked like they were about to lose bodily function, as did my children.

We rested by a tree with a Chinese pagoda behind us. I took the opportunity to take a photograph. My family looked miserable, except Carrie who gave a caustic smile. If it was not for the fact that I held the cash and had the power of purchase of a cold coke, then there would have been mutiny on the soporific slopes of Marble Mountain.

We drove the final miles into Hoi An at the pace of a funeral cortege. The road bordered empty plots of baked earth and weeds in a scene that went on for miles. We assumed the area would eventually become hotels since the beaches at the far end of the empty plots looked idyllic. The desolation left us bored and the only subject that Mary and I felt inspired to talk about was Danang speed limits. We had this conversation with an enthusiasm for such matters that seems to come with middle age. With the air conditioning on full pelt, we all froze in the back. It felt like torture and we were desperate for the tour to end.

@@@@@

All tension was quickly forgotten at Hoi An. The hotel was twice the price as the one in Ben Tre, but it was a price worth paying with neat two-storey accommodation blocks surrounding a pool and a verdant garden of manicured tropical flowers. We had two adjoining rooms furnished with teak furniture and a bed that was large enough to sleep an entire minibus of people who like to starfish. Best of all, the air conditioning was under our control and so we made it cool enough that we were comfortable, but not so cold that fleeces were required.

Evan turned on the television and watched a Vietnamese children's show, Carrie and Rueben took the opportunity to run around the room naked, and Mary washed our tropically-soaked underpants.

Throughout the day, Evan kept scratching his tongue against his teeth like a lizard tasting the air. He said he was trying to quell an itch in his mouth that never went away. I looked inside his mouth at the hotel and saw white spots that Google images suggested was oral thrush.

That evening we walked three kilometres into town along a tree-lined boulevard washed clean by a monsoon shower. Evan walked with his head down and looked like he wanted to cry, a matter made worse when I reluctantly forced him into a local chemist to purchase something for his tongue. The shopkeeper grabbed his jaw to make him open it and then squinted inside his mouth as if she were looking through a keyhole. She gave us some drops to place on his tongue and even though the instructions were in Vietnamese, it cleared up the infection after a few applications.

By the time we reached town, we were tired and so immediately looked for a place to eat. We entered an undercover market the size of several tennis courts, with neat rows of benches and makeshift kitchens all selling local Vietnamese cuisine for the price of a fun-size chocolate bar. The walls looked covered in oily grime from years of smoking fat and the concrete floor was worn smooth from footfall. All the places looked the same and so choosing a place to sit gave me a conundrum.

"Should we go where other Westerners were eating? Does that look like we're afraid and looking for safety in numbers or that the vendor can speak good English but cook rubbish food and charge a premium price? Do we sit at a bench where no one is sitting? However, if no one is sitting there, is that because the cook has an excellent record of poisoning people?"

All these thoughts raced around my head. Looking back, it was a simple and insignificant decision. Perhaps it was my lingering cold and tiredness that made me so indecisive. We walked down all the rows and faced deciding immediately or walking out of the hall.

Halfway up the final row, we found a place where no Westerners sat, but some locals seemed to be enjoying a meal. I decided that this was the place. We sat on aluminium benches facing a woman who took our order and prepared our food. Rueben only wanted chops. Carrie, Mary and I had delicious bowls of Cao Lau (bowls of rice noodles and broth with strips of pork placed on top). Evan ate plain chicken and rice and ate it all even though he grimaced at every mouthful. He ate under duress and the watchful eye of Mary exploding at him again, just like she did at the airport earlier that day.

Eating at Hoi An indoor market

The woman who served us wore a dress shaped like a sack and sweat made her hair stick to her forehead. Even though she looked tired, she moved effortlessly around her kitchen, and joked and smiled with the women around her. As Rueben and Carrie ate, she whispered gentle and unknown syllables that sounded a bit like purring to them, and she stroked Rueben's hair. She reminded me of a happy and experienced mother.

After dinner, we wandered towards the riverfront. On the quay, there was a ferry full of motorbikes and people. Behind them lightning exploded out of a cumulus cloud but no one on the ferry seemed to notice. They all looked bored and tired and reminded me of the army of London Underground commuters I saw on my daily commute to the office.

On the roads leading away from the riverfront, market vendors laid fresh vegetables out on tables or rugs on the pavements. We purchased some rambutan and doughnuts cooked fresh at the stall. The young mother who served us took great delight in Rueben and spoke with Mary about her own four-year-old son. Mary was confused because the doughnut seller kept on speaking about her son but showing her a picture of a child in a dress, but Mary smiled and nodded her head as if in complete comprehension.

@@@@@

The following morning the children could not wait to get into the pool and insisted on a swim before breakfast. I sat on the side of the pool drinking my first coffee of the day watching Evan and Rueben. Rueben decided to practice kicking in the water next to some French retirees having breakfast, splashing pool water into their coffee. I thought about the visit to Sri Lanka the year before and Rueben's near miss when he jumped over a

French woman, and I wondered if he had a special gene that made him behave inappropriately towards French people near swimming pools.

Breakfast tasted delicious, though the children kept changing their minds and confused our waitress. We ended up with six plates of cooked eggs, four coffees even though we ordered two, and six plates of fresh fruit for five people (much to Rueben's dismay).

"So, what are we going to do today, Dad?" Evan asked.

"We'll go for a walk around the town." I responded.

"You are joking, aren't you?" Carrie retorted and banged her coffee cup down.

"Aren't you too young to be drinking coffee?" I asked, hoping to change the subject of the conversation.

Judging by the folded arms from Rueben and the fallen bottom lip from Evan, I think my children took the news about a walk in the heat to look at old buildings about as well as they would have had I told them that they were no longer allowed chocolate until they are old enough to buy alcohol.

Unsurprisingly, Carrie, Rueben and Evan dragged out getting ready and we finally got into the town an hour later than we hoped, and by then the sun made me feel that I was going to chafe badly. Rueben had the same concern and complained about the sweat that dripped down his crack and made his bottom sting.

Hoi An was never attacked by the opposing sides in the Vietnam War and this meant that the trading town was left largely intact. It used to be a major port that brought the Japanese, Chinese, Portuguese and Dutch to trade in spices. They all built homes, temples and meeting houses. All these places were built according to their own nationalistic tastes where they could show off their own culture or relax in a space that reminded them of their native homes. The beautiful spaces they created attract tourists now that the spice has moved on. When we visited, the place was full of backpackers after a bargain, and bored or overweight Chinese tourists getting pedalled around the ancient streets in cycle rickshaws, but that did not take away anything from the place.

That morning, we wandered through the old town. Mary and I admired ancient honeycomb-coloured houses and the bougainvillea that formed pleasant shelters for many of the shop fronts. Carrie stormed in front; enthused by the shops selling trinkets and t-shirts (that in my experience always shrink to half the size on the first wash), and the possibility of buying something like a Non-La hat or a lacquered coconut shell for her friends back in the UK.

Canned electrical music piped through loud speakers in a scene reminiscent of 'One Flew Over The Cuckoo's Nest'. After a few minutes, our t-shirts were soaked with sweat. We went into some of the key buildings that made this place a UNESCO world heritage site such as the 'Assembly Hall of the Fujian Chinese congregation', 'Museum of Trading Ceramic', 'Assembly of Hainan Chinese Congregation' and a covered Japanese bridge that was meant to be famous, but I think looked a little squalid and not at all photogenic. Carrie and Evan engaged in the first place, we visited and enjoyed looking at the large bells, garish brass dragons, ceilings painted the colours of an ice cream parlour and enormous wooden chandeliers. After the first place though, they were bored and usually looked around for a few seconds, sighed in disappointment and wallowed in the shade. Rueben, however, ran around the Chinese dragons, the life size garish horse statues, the model boats complete with rigging displayed next to alters and the fish in the ponds in the surrounding gardens like the place was a toy shop.

At the end of the walk, we were all so hot and thirsty that we devoured cold cokes with a fervour rarely seen outside pie-eating competitions.

In the evening, we returned to the same stall run by the woman who liked to stroke Rueben, and ate the same food. She seemed more pleased to be serving Rueben again rather than seeing us as a returning business opportunity. We confused her when we all applauded Evan as he opened a can of coke. He is a great footballer but has as much strength in his hands as a feather.

After dinner, we walked around the market and Carrie chose a lacquered bowl and a pen holder as a reward for her efforts earlier in the day.

"I have no change. Give change tomorrow," the woman said smiling at me as she handed over the pen holder.

I laughed. "How about I come and pay tomorrow?"

I was quite pleased with my comeback line.

The interior of the temples at Hoi An

@@@@@

Having just avoided seriously annoying the children with the walk around Hoi An, Mary and I wanted to find something that would engage them. 'Jackie Tran's eco tour' was easily the most expensive tour I have ever paid for. It cost around seventy-five dollars per person, but it was exactly what we were looking for and worth every penny. At precisely eight o'clock (as promised on the leaflet), a spotless minibus picked us up. It was a sign of the attention to detail that carried on for the rest of the tour. We drove to the outskirts of the town and met two guides who stood guard with the exact number of required bikes, including a baby seat for Rueben and a back seat for Evan. After a few minutes of cycling along paddy fields, we came across a large flock of ducklings cared for by a man whose skin was covered in deep cracks that looked like scars, but I suspect was caused by a lifetime's exposure to the sun. As we passed by, the ducklings flocked to him in fear, much to Rueben and Carrie's surprise because they thought the man with cracked skin looked terrifying. I thought it ironic that their surrogate parent that they turned to for protection would eventually hand them over for butchering.

We cycled to a market garden where an old woman showed us how they gathered seaweed from the coast, allowed it to be naturally washed in the rain and used as fertilizer. The neat lines of lettuce, spring onions, Thai mint and basil were beautiful to look at. All adults had an opportunity to water the plant rows using watering cans balanced on a bamboo pole resting on their shoulders. The thing that I remember so much about our guide at the garden was her amazing flexibility. At the age of eighty, she bent down to plant vegetables with straight legs and appeared to have a natural core strength I have only seen in toddlers. I knew if I bent down as she did

113

then something internal would break that would only heal with a firm rubbing from a physiotherapist and a hefty dose of drugs. I made a mental note to begin palates when I returned to the UK. The children enjoyed planting vegetables with her and the woman stroked Carrie's hair and spoke words and syllables that we could not understand, but her tone was kind and her stroke gentle and so Carrie smiled as if she had been given a present.

We cycled on a short while and stopped next to a water buffalo. The owner ran towards us as we approached. He had a moustache that reminded me of 'Lenny' from 'Motorhead', and I suspected he was a little drunk. All paying tourists took turns riding on the buffalo as he sang and waved his hat around like a loved-up matador. I rode with Evan and Rueben. Riding a buffalo was like straddling a gently rocking hot barrel that smelt like fish. Getting onto a buffalo is much more challenging and a young Austrian woman ended up lying across the beast like a human blanket much to our amusement and her embarrassment. The man she was with added salt to her embarrassment by running up and straddling it in a single bound. I was later tempted to compliment the embarrassed woman (who I thought was his girlfriend) on how lucky she was to have such an agile partner. However, I was thankful I refrained from such discourse because later that day he explained the woman was in fact his sister. The children all loved riding the buffalo as the beast wobbled across the baked hard fields caused by the sizzling heat.

Whilst we waited to ride the animal, a calf came forward through curiosity. There is a magnetism between Carrie and baby animals and she gave it a stroke. It responded by giving a firm lick of Carrie's legs with its rough tongue.

"Dad, will I get rabies now?" she asked,

"No," I paused as I took a photo. "Well I don't

think so," I responded reassuringly and made a note to look for any mouth frothing over the next few days.

The calf turned its attention to Mary and tried to stick its nose up her dress, making her shriek. Then it turned its attention to Rueben who was wearing a red top. Rueben turned and fled.

"Yes! You are wearing perfect bull-fighting colour!" Sinh, our guide, shouted as he laughed at Rueben's flight.

After the buffalo, we cycled on and took a leisurely cruise across the estuary to a plantation of water coconuts transplanted from the Mekong Delta three hundred years before. The plantations were an ideal haven for fishing boats when typhoons hit and were a great place to hide when ambushing Americans in the war. The Americans promptly retaliated to such ambushes and bombed the plantations. Fifty years later, the resulting craters in the groves had been converted into ramshackle fish farms and harbours.

Carrie and Evan with the water buffalo

We toured the groves in coracles and stopped for the guides to tear off palm leaves. They took the leaves and folded them into necklaces, hats, glasses and even a grasshopper. However, it was the wildlife that grabbed the children's attention as they floated amongst the trees. Carrie was particularly pleased with seven crabs caught by her guide. They had purple claws that were not much bigger than the diameter of a plum.

Back on the boat and perfectly orchestrated like everything on the tour, we passed an elderly couple on a fishing boat. The woman sat impassive as the man threw in a large net that opened perfectly just as we passed. The click of cameras that belonged to the touring party reminded me of the noise moments after a world leader appears to make press statement.

Carrie and the calf

That evening, having built up cycling confidence on

the tour, we borrowed bikes from the hotel and rode into town. In the relative cool of sunset, the roads were crowded with locals and other tourists on bikes. We passed markets selling fruits of which only half I could name, and stalls where bored looking locals casually gouged the innards of cut-up animals whilst scanning the passers-by; hoping someone would stop and buy their carved-up meat.

We returned to our friendly woman to eat Cau Lau and rice. Like the previous day, she was thrilled to see Rueben and even purchased some bananas and presented them to him as a gift. It did nothing to improve his diet and Mary and I ate them the next day. If anything, her kindness made matters worse because this attention made Rueben feel entitled to pick and choose what he ate.

He refused to eat anything unless Carrie fed him, and only if she pretended the spoon was an aeroplane. I was impressed by Carrie's kindness, but she did have a stake in making him eat because I said there would be no doughnuts after dinner unless all three finished their food. That evening, I left the indoor market with a full belly, a deep sense of happiness and a bunch of bananas.

@@@@@

The next day we went to Cua Dai beach. It was the nearest beach to the hotel and was stunning; golden sands and palm trees formed a backdrop to azure waters. Rueben initially refused to go into the sea but when he saw Carrie and Evan jumping and waving their arms in unbridled joy as they raced into the water, he turned on Mum and chided her for not getting him ready quick enough.

"Mum, seriously you need to be quick."

As he came out of the water, a wave of goodness washed over him, and he declared that he would never be naughty again to his Mother.

Whilst we were on a beach in Vietnam, Evan's mind was elsewhere.

"Dad was Ben Nevis named after someone called Ben?", "Dad, what is higher – Scafell Pike or Snowden?" and "Dad, have you ever been in the death zone? Like on Everest?"

As I wandered over to the water for a final swim, he shouted out, "Dad, I've built Snowden, Tryfan and the Glyders in the sand. Are there any other mountains in Snowdonia I can build?"

When I came back, mountains from all over Great Britain sat as sand mounds and Evan guided me around them with pride. Five minutes later a skeletal dog the size of a handbag took a prompt sniff of Ben Nevis and urinated on its side, causing a significant collapse.

Mary and Rueben at Cua Dai beach

We relaxed in the shade and drank cold cokes as

the children played around us. A hawker named Lin came and sat with us. Normally we sent hawkers away with an irritated swish of the hand and perhaps a scowl, but she sounded so tired and gentle that Mary and I chatted with her about her children who were aged around Carrie and Evan's age. We think she said that she only hawked at the weekend and that her husband had gone crazy. She told us all this through sign language as she drew air circles around her ears, and then stuck her thumb in her mouth (I was not certain if the thumb sucking meant he behaved like a child or that he drank too much moonshine). Either way we purchased many wares from her including a greetings card of a pop-up woman in traditional Vietnamese dress on a bicycle and some dragonflies that balanced perfectly on our fingers.

As the sun strengthened into the heat of the day, we returned to the hotel and rested. Rueben fell asleep but woke up bucking and kicking, crying as if his life was too much for him to bear. Carrie and Evan watched cartoons that contained a character that looked like a green blob with bulbous eyes and spoke only Vietnamese. They watched with absolute focus - as if it were a country leader announcing a war. I noticed that Evan looked like he had slapped cheeks and Carrie had tan lines across her buttock that looked the colour of raspberries. We used factor fifty cream and promised ourselves that our children would not burn, but they still returned with their red features.

On the way to dinner, we cycled around Hoi An for the last time. It was a lovely experience as we looked out at fishing boats squatting in the mud. We rode past locals wearing Non-La hats. Most rode bikes that squeaked with age and, as the sun set, they created shadows that were larger than the buildings and looked cartoonish.

We ate for the last time with our woman in the market. Despite spending four nights eating her food and sitting on her benches, I did not know her name. That evening, she told us her name was Lan, and the lady who served us drinks from the stall opposite was called Thanh. After we ate our food, Lan gave Rueben a gentle squeeze and despite Rueben's objections, she lifted Rueben up so that I could take a photo. As we walked away, she waved at us.

"Wishing good luck!" she shouted. She was not satisfied with this departure and as we waved, she called us over and embraced each of us with a warm hug.

Chapter 3: Ninh Binh and Nguyen Shack

A taxi came to take us to the train station in Danang for an overnight train to Ninh Binh. At first, we drove and followed signs to Danang, but to our surprise the driver took a bypass and headed out towards countryside. I thought it a bit odd that the station was so far out of town, but I trusted his judgement. A few minutes later, however, I saw the tail of a plane and realised that he thought we wanted to go to the airport.

Mary tried explaining that it was the train station we needed. However, with the driver looking confused, she resorted to charades and moved her arms like a train and said 'choo choo'. After a minute of stifled giggles from the children in the back and Mary's confused movements, I thought it best to try a different tact and pulled the tickets out of our bag. He instantly recognised his mistake, pointed at Mary, laughed and turned the car around.

"Say lula!" He repeated several times, laughing.

At the time I wondered if he was suggesting that Mary's attempt to communicate was something akin to a village idiot, but having looked at translations after the fact, I think he was saying 'train' in Vietnamese.

We had plenty of time to get to the station and so the trip to the airport seemed more amusing than stressful. However, the moment we turned onto the main road in Danang, there was gridlock. The driver looked concerned.

"This is not normal," he said.

After ten minutes of crawling, I saw the reason for the delay. Roads in Vietnam have some of the highest death rates in the world and so far, we had seen no incidents, but in Danang that ended. A man was hit or knocked off a bike and wore no helmet. Blood poured from the back of his head and he was not moving. It looked serious bordering on helpless. I kept the children's attention away by pointing out things on the other side of the road, but Evan was not to be distracted and had a good look as we passed.

"Wow there's a lot of blood here, Dad."

His remark was so casual, it was if he was making a comment about a carpet of weeds that needed to be pulled up in a vegetable patch. I watched for signs of any distress but saw none in Evan and as soon as we reached the station, Rueben and he continued their favourite game of inflicting maximum incapacitation by head-butting or kicking each other in the balls.

Our train was waiting when we arrived and so we immediately boarded. We felt like we had entered the 1970s, with walls of brown veneer and chocolate-coloured leather benches that doubled up as beds. Regardless of décor, most important of all, the carriages looked clean. As we trundled off, we opened a packet of crisps that Evan insisted we purchased called Swing. On the packaging, it said they were hot Pacific-flavoured crisps and they tasted like fishy cardboard, but with a peppery aftertaste. Because of these crisps, whenever I think of this journey, I can still taste fish and pepper.

We settled in for the night. Carrie sat on the top bunk sucking on a pen and smiled as if she was reading a love letter, Evan lay on the bunk below reading a book called 'Football Academy', and Mary and Rueben drew houses. I sat and wrote, but kept on getting distracted by the view that flew by outside; a vista of rice paddies, water buffalo, and thin strips of land crowded with ducks. In the distance, steep limestone hills with rounded and forested peaks sat in silhouette as the sun set behind them. The view was stunning. I put my pen down to take in the beauty but only had a few seconds of peace before I had to deal with a tantrum from Rueben. Mary suggested he wrote the word 'house' above his drawing, but this suggestion made him throw the pen down and wear a pillow over his head in defiance.

Night drew in and so I took the children to the toilet. The small cupboard-shaped room was as damp as a swimming pool changing room and the only way to clean up after having a poo was to use a pressurised hose. Rueben and Evan shrieked in delight at using the hose as a water gun, but Carrie was less certain and decided she would wait until we arrived at our next hotel.

The train trundled into the night on its sedate journey up north. We should have all slept well, and I think the children did. However, just as I turned off a light, a cockroach the length of a clothes peg scarpered under the bed by Rueben's foot. In the darkness my feet started to itch. I was convinced the itch was caused by the light-footed insects searching for food.

That morning I woke up early. We still had a few hours before we were due to arrive in Ninh Binh and so, with Rueben asleep, I took Carrie and Evan to the restaurant car for breakfast. There was nothing on the menu that appealed to them, but I purchased a bowl of rice soup. It tasted like salty wallpaper paste with lumps of chicken dispersed through the mass. Before we left for Vietnam, I read that we needed to plan for delays and dirtiness on the trains. However, as I sat and ate the rice soup and looked out at countryside lit up by the early morning light, I was full and utterly satisfied with the whole experience. I was so impressed, I even purchased a Vietnam railways t-shirt. It is one of the few garments that I purchased from this area of the world that has not shrunk in the wash.

@@@@@

In the late afternoon, I sat in a hammock in a bamboo shack built out over a lake that looked like it was losing a battle against pond weed, but that did not make the surroundings any less beautiful. Grey limestone cliffs covered in jungle foliage soared above and around the shack in a natural amphitheatre. I put down my pen and paper and soaked up the views. Behind me, Carrie leant on a cane coffee table and drew, Evan lay on the sofa and read a book called 'Demolition Man' and Rueben played the drums using chopsticks; wiggling his bottom in time to his self-made rhythm.

I thought about the day so far. Whenever Rueben was present at the communal dining room, the proprietors treated him like a rock star. They kissed, prodded, chased, cuddled, swung and threw the boy into the air. A pregnant woman named Zuna, her husband Noname and Zuna's cousin Lam ran the place with such joy it was as if there was a permanent party.

They had a pet pig called Bacon and a dog called Coco. When we first arrived, Coco had thick hair that hung over her eyes and a tongue that constantly hung out of her mouth. Evan thought the tongue made her look like she was sucking on a pink smoking pipe.

I lay in the hammock and thought about our first ten minutes at Nguyen Shack. We had only just placed our bags on the floor when an Australian woman with a drawling accent, short hair and tattoos came to our table and introduced herself as Nina. I was pleasantly surprised by this because so far, no tourists really spoke with us unless we spoke to them first. We chatted with Nina about Vietnam and about Coco who sat nearby, panting. Nina thought it too hot for a dog to have such a thick coat and so, after some discussion with the owners, scissors appeared where in most normal circumstances, only coffees would be requested and delivered.

"Trust me, I'm a nurse," she said and winked at us.

I never understand comments like this. If I had an open wound that required a dressing, I would never resort to a dog groomer or a barber to bandage it up.

We were there for only ten minutes and were still drinking refreshing complimentary drinks that were given as part of our welcome when we saw Coco buck and fight as she had her haircut. It all added spice to the madness.

Minutes later, Lam came over, sat with us, and took a second look at Coco. Coco looked at Lam, turned around and faced the wall, seemingly sulking that she was now bald.

"Ah, Coco you now have lovely hair like Lam! Be happy!"

Lam had a hair style that would befit a K-pop star. He walked with a slight swagger and smiled the whole time. He was the showman and entertainer of Nguyen Shack and the core of much of the madness and laughter. If Vietnam needed their own Willy Wonka, then Lam would be a perfect fit.

"Hey, you three, come let's fish!" He spoke to the children like he was a quiz show host and beckoned them to follow him with a theatrical sweep of his arm.

True to his word, he showed my children how to fish in the lake using a simple bamboo pole, some bread and a hook. I thought such rudimentary fishing was only possible in novels written by Mark Twain and I was sceptical that they would catch anything, but it gave them great joy. I was not going to interfere or knock their efforts and was happy to sit down, write my diary and rest. Once Carrie and Evan were competent fishers, Lam turned his attention to Rueben and chased him around pretending to be Coco; picking him up and feeding him to Bacon the pig. The screams came before the fall, however, and Rueben tripped over a chair leg and scraped his knees. Mary and I had to calm the situation down. Lam was kind, full of life and utterly mad.

After Rueben's accident, I thought it was best to be in the peace and quiet of the shack, but the children thought sitting around in the quiet room was a total waste of time. They were desperate to get back to the action. After a night sleeping on the train and the heat, I did not understand where the children got their energy. I was concerned they would crash and burn and needed some time away from the delightful madhouse and Lam's company.

"Dad please can we go back to the dining room?" Carrie pleaded.

It was obvious they would rather crash and burn than sit with Mum and Dad.

"Go on," I said after a short pause.

Only Carrie asked, but Evan and Rueben piled out after her. I tried to write but was distracted by a grasshopper lifted by two flying ants making their way along the bamboo floor. Part of me wondered if it was a mercy mission, but I suspected it was a successful hunting trip. From the communal dining room, I heard the yelps and laughter of my children and saw Carrie throw out a line from a bamboo rod.

"She looks so sweet even though it's utterly futile," I remarked to Mary, who was also looking over at our eldest daughter.

"It is so lovely here," Mary said as she joined me in a hammock.

A breeze blew off the water and made the reeds in the pond rustle. It refreshed me and made me feel very sleepy. Writing was too hard in that condition and so I dropped my pen and paper, cuddled Mary and closed my eyes.

Suddenly there was a great shout of acclamation

from the dining room. I sat up instantly and saw Carrie pulling on the pole. Instinct took over as I leapt out of the hammock and instantly woke Mary with my efforts; almost tipping her out of the hammock. I am sure I heard her shout at me in shock as I ran out of the shack and up the suspended bamboo walkway. When I arrived, I saw Lam helping Carrie unhook a fish the size of her hand. Rueben watched nearby with his mouth open. He was so shocked at the flapping animal at the end of the rod that he fled back to the hut, much to the amusement of the owners who chased him with the gulping fish.

Carrie fishing at Nguyen Shack

Nguyen Shack was a wonderful place. It was in beautiful surroundings, it was run by some of the happiest people I encountered in Vietnam who loved my children, but the nicest thing about the place was that it had a social conscience. Each evening, the local children, dressed in anything from summer dresses to filthy stained vests, sat at school desks in a shelter built next to Bacon's enclosure. Once all present and seated, the children spent thirty minutes with Lam or a hotel guest and learnt English. That evening, I agreed to run an English lesson with Lam. I had never taught English before and had no idea what to expect and so as I stood in front of a group of ten children aged five to seven, I had no idea what to do.

David teaching 'ing' words – probably running, perhaps dancing

"I know, let's have a game of hangman!" I exclaimed. I was conscious I sounded like a scary children's television presenter, but in my defence, I was very nervous.

Lam looked at me with wide eyes and shook his head. I took it from his body language that I had just suggested something equivalent to 'spin the bottle' in a school. I needed to think on my feet.

"I know, let's play charades and learn some action words!" I wrote the words on a blackboard and then started charades. This time I was the object of stifled giggles from my family as I led a game of charades,f doing 'ing' words. The children guessed sleeping, jumping and walking, but struggled with dying even though my theatrical death was worthy of an award. I looked at the local children as I fell on the floor and groaned, and they looked at me in confusion mixed with alarm. Clearly people died differently in Vietnam.

Later that evening, we borrowed bikes and cycled just five hundred metres to a hill that had three hundred and fifty steep steps to the top. Once there, our guidebook said we would be rewarded with magnificent views over the Tam Coc river. I am always a sucker for views, but I knew the family found stairs that ascend hills in Asia a source of great despondency. Yet again, the only way I could carry on would be if I carried Rueben all the way to the top.

My heart felt like it was about to burst out of its socket and pulsate like the bucking and dying fish that Carrie caught earlier. However, our guidebook was right and the view on the top was spectacular with flat lincoln green fields and enormous jungle-clad limestone tablets popping out of the earth. I considered the scenery stunning and took photos whilst the others sat on the steps drenched in sweat, held their heads in their hands and scowled. It was not that they did not think the scenery also stunning; it was just that they did not consider the view worth a coronary.

In the park at the bottom of the hill were life-sized concrete horses and a few smiling male statues with closed eyes, like they just had a satisfying poo. These pleased Rueben immensely and left Carrie rolling her eyes in bored irritation.

"Can we go now Dad?" she whined.

I saw a muddy signpost labelled 'Tam Coc viewpoint'. The path promised a view of the river and so whilst Mary and Carrie thought such effort after the hill climb was an anathema, the boys and I walked down the gravelled path. The path quickly morphed into puddles and the air was full of mosquitoes. We pressed on hoping that our way would get better or that we would soon reach the river but gave up when we were forced to walk through ankle-deep mud. The mud stained my sandals so badly that even after three days and a lot of washing they still looked like I fished them out of a portable toilet at a festival.

The view at the top of Tam Coc viewpoint – note the joyful demeanour of the family.

@@@@@

The next day, after a very long sleep and a relaxing breakfast, we cycled across wasteland with a grey coloured concrete factory in the distance that towered over the countryside; uncompromising and brutal. I thought it odd that somewhere between the factory and us was a stunning stretch of river that attracts crowds of tourists. As I cycled in the heat and noticed the children beginning to wilt, I thought it so odd that I became uncertain that we were travelling in the right direction. Because we got up late and we had a relaxing breakfast, the day was entering its hottest part and I knew if we were lost, that we would need to head back to Nguyen Shack or face the possibility of a child suffering with heat stroke.

"Let's stop," I stated.

I tried to sound calm as I pulled over in a thin slice of shade on the road to ascertain where we were on a mud map supplied by our crazy hosts.

"Are you lost?" Mary asked.

"No, no," I responded. "I just don't want to get lost."

"Great, we're lost," Carrie muttered.

"We're not lost. I'm just a bit unsure of where we are. There is a difference."

Some children approached us; unsmiling and curious.

"Tam Coc?" I said.

They pointed down the road and waved us on.

"See, I knew we were not lost."

I smiled at my family though they did not smile back. I think they were all hoping we were lost so we could return to Nguyen Shack and drink ice cold lime juice.

After a few kilometres of cycling, we arrived at the Tam Coc river, but we were all tomato-coloured. Evan particularly looked febrile with his peeling skin and soaking wet brow.

Local women sized us up and then assigned us our

boats (boys in one and girls in the other) and pedalled (I say pedalled because the rowers used their feet to power their oars) along a river that meandered through caves and amazing countryside, with tablet-shaped limestone karsts towering above. Mary and Carrie travelled in their boat ahead of us, and they sheltered under an umbrella and looked like they had civilised conversations. I, however, had Evan and Rueben who enjoyed the first ten minutes but soon afterwards made groaning sounds and hit each other out of boredom.

We paddled through three caves and at the end entered a large pond where we turned around and dealt with a fearsome army of female sellers on boats sinking under the weight of lollipops, fruit and cold drinks. The sellers tried to make me purchase a cold drink for our drivers. A firm 'no' and a disinterested look was required to deny our pedalling women and their hawkers. I felt guilty that I did not buy drinks, but I did tip them generously when we got back to dry land. On the return journey, my pedalling lady did not stop chatting away even when her companion was tens of meters down the river. She was like a chicken with an irritation, and I wondered if my refusal to purchase from the sellers had made her this way. The other driver looked sternly ahead as our driver gabbled on. Even the unbelievable heat did nothing to sedate her whereas Evan, Rueben and I melted like margarine in a hot pan.

The boys and I sat silently in the boat. Evan reached in to the bag and pulled out some bubble gum.

"Dad, you know the lady who cut Coco's hair and was from Australia?" Evan asked as he unwrapped the gum.

"Yes," I responded.

"Well she called a yoghurt 'yoge hurts' at breakfast. Do you think she would call apples 'ape balls?'" he asked.

I sighed, unsure of how to answer such a question in the heat and watched him lift the unwrapped gum into his mouth. He did not grip it properly and it dropped into the pond below; floating silently away to be a treat for the river fish.

Carrie and Mary on the Tam Coc River

After the morning activities on the river, we had no strength to do anything in the afternoon and so we relaxed around Nguyen Shack. I sat in a hammock overlooking the pond in our hut and wrote my diary. Suddenly I heard shouts that could only herald a small child falling in the pond or the capturing of a carp. Either way it left me running to the source of excitement. When I arrived, Lam stood next to Carrie and suddenly there was a surge and a black shadow in the water. Lam spoke in whispers to the other owners, who quickly went to the kitchen and returned with bowls. I detected that this was not a normal event.

Carrie caught a fish that was the length of a rolling pin and judging by the interest of the owners, this was a rare event. We watched with cameras readied and mouths open as the cook cut open the fish and removed the innards that were army green and sausage shaped. Some of the anatomy she removed looked a little like a puffed-up bag and made Carrie giggle because she thought it looked like something rude. Suddenly the ancient cook brought the knife straight through the mouth of the fish and slit its head in two. This happened just as I took a photo. Blood spattered across my ankles that was immediately licked by a local cat. Carrie squealed in shock and Rueben shrieked in delight.

Lam with Carrie and her catch

That evening we ate Carrie's catch stewed in ginger and garlic. It was immensely bony and had the consistency of slimy lard. However, it was my daughter's first proper catch and I was very proud. In my mind, it was a king's feast.

@@@@@

Rodents and family disturbed my sleep that night. It started with Mary. She woke me at around midnight to tell me she heard small animals dancing on a crisp packet.

"Great, though could the news have perhaps waited until daybreak?" I suggested gently.

At that point I was tolerant of interruptions and fell asleep quickly, but it was not to last.

For the next five hours I slept well, but at five o'clock I awoke to see a mouse running along a joist. I lay in bed and tried to sleep but was kept awake by the irrational thought that mice were the favourite food of snakes in this part of the world, and if rodents were running around the shack, then soon there would be cobras on the hunt. With that concern I lay in bed until six o'clock; alert and listening for any noises that indicated reptiles had invaded. My eyes burned with tiredness.

As the sun began to rise, I fell into a light slumber. That too was not to last.

Suddenly, Rueben fell out of bed and landed on Carrie's clock. His cries echoed around the cliffs. Mary and I jumped out of bed, made sure he was not badly hurt and gave him cuddles to calm his howls, but the damage was done, and Evan and Carrie (and probably most of the other guests) were awake and ready to start the day.

"Dad, I'm hungry," Evan said.

"We've got an hour before we can go for breakfast, but there might be some bread on the coffee table," I mumbled as I turned around in bed and gave Rueben a cuddle.

I hoped everyone would fall back to sleep again and was disappointed to hear Evan climb out of bed.

"Dad!" Evan screamed.

I shot up, convinced that there was a cobra. To my surprise, blood pooled on the bamboo floor.

"What have you done!" I shouted at Evan, half in tired shock, half in fear.

"I cut my toe on that nail," he wailed and pointed to a protruding nail just by his bed.

As Evan limped around unsure of where to go or what to do, he turned the shack into a scene that looked like an amateur butcher's shop. Within seconds, there were spatters all over the floor and even on the coffee table. I was shocked that so much blood could come from a big toe.

"Well don't walk around like that, go and wash it in the bathroom!", I hollered.

The lack of sleep and the calamities that fell upon my children left me feeling very grumpy. I looked over to Mary after we dressed and tidied up the blood. Her eyes were puffy, and she looked like she had just starred in a disaster movie. When Mary and I are tired, it always creates a perfect storm for disharmony. Both of us looked ready to turn on each other but, unexpectedly, Mary laughed.

"Dave, you look like you are ready for the knacker's yard," she said and drew me in for a cuddle.

I was so glad she did that for two reasons; cuddles are always welcome in my world, but also it gave me a few moments to remember that coming to Vietnam and staying in these places was mostly my idea. I needed to lead rather than shout.

After a breakfast of baguette, bacon, eggs and fruit juice, I commandeered some bikes again. The children sensed that I was in no mood to deal with complaints and gave me a wide berth, though I think Mary may have had to deal with some whinging that bikes were to feature again in the day's activities. Even Lam (who promised to help in adjusting seats on the bikes) sensed my tiredness, made his excuses and went to play with my son. Whilst I battled the bikes, I heard Rueben whoop with joy and Lam make monkey noises. Entertaining small children was clearly more desirable for Lam than undoing nuts with me.

Rueben on a bike near Nguyen Shack

We cycled on empty country roads full of potholes and past ducks that seemed to prefer existing in a state of nervous anxiety in the road rather than wallowing in the baby poo-green waters of the paddy fields. Eventually we arrived at the main road that took us to Hua Lu. The road was wide, empty of cars, asphalted and meandered around the tablet-shaped hills and through tunnels. It made me think it would be an amazing backdrop for a road race. In the heat and in my delirium, I made a mental note to write to the Vietnamese High Commission in London and suggest this. When I remarked to Lam how good the road was, he laughed and said the only people who travelled on that road were tourists.

If we had a time machine and travelled back in time around one thousand years, then Hua Lu would have been a thriving centre of commerce, kingship and culture. It was the main capital before Hanoi but today, almost nothing remains. We arrived covered in sweat and wondered why we bothered. I felt slightly cheated, as if I climbed a mountain only for the cloud to pile in just as I summited. The scant ruins were a desolate place, surrounded by hills and with vast wide roads that looked wide enough to land an aircraft. There was a pagoda stranded in what looked like a car park and other buildings sat behind a purple tarpaulin that made the ruins look makeshift and temporary. Our guidebook suggested that we walk up to a grave of a long dead king for a perspective of the area. Rueben, Evan and I set off across the paddy fields but within minutes were forced back by a gang of enthusiastic dogs.

Just down the road was Am Tien Pagoda, but the gates were locked and by the time I climbed the weed covered marble steps to pull on the door, Carrie had her bike facing towards the road. In the heat, it was clear which way she wanted to go.

We arrived back at Nguyen Shack in the hottest part of the day and drank coke and fresh lime juice. Lam led the children to a cave where they spotted bats and saw the orange flash of a monkey. The caves were mud-brown and full of mosquitoes, but they were cool and provided a relief to the sweaty heat. The children took me to the caves later that afternoon and I stood feeling immensely relieved in the cool but prayed that God would not send an earthquake at that moment, nor that any mosquitoes that buzzed around my face would be malarial.

That evening Mary and I sat in hammocks, drank

beer, saw fireflies, marvelled at the stars and hoped the rain that we smelt would fall and cool us all. However, all we got were power cuts and insufferable heat that made us all miserable. Nguyen Shack was great, but we could not wait to get back to the luxury of air-conditioning.

The beautiful staff at Nguyen Shack

Chapter 4: Halong Bay

On the road, motorcycles bumped along the hard shoulder; some carried towering sacks of rice placed on the back rack, some carried piglets kept in crude looking barrels and one even carried goldfish inside plastic bags that stacked up high in the shape of a tree. We passed huge shipyards and factories that pumped out black smoke and others that covered the road and surrounding houses in a red dust. Rueben sat on my lap in the front in the taxi to Halong City and his weight as he slept made my right buttock ache so badly that it gave me an image of a rusty nail imbedded into my coccyx. No amount of buttock clenching relieved me.

Entering Halong City made me feel like I made a mistake. On one side of the road, huge hotels that would not look out of place in Benidorm towered over us. On the other side, a bay sealed off by a high construction fence blocked the view of the sea. Lorries drove past us spraying water on the road to stifle the dust from the construction and ended up creating banks of mud that made the road look like it recently flooded.

"Dear God, help our hotel to be much further away from this horrible place," I prayed.

Thirty seconds later, the taxi driver pulled over at "Paradise Bay Hotel".

Our shoes were caked in mud from our time in Nguyen Shack and I became conscious in the clean air of the huge marble lobby that we smelt like a neglected armpit. I tried to enter quietly; hoping our smell and filthy shoes would not be noticed. My children, however, had other ideas. Rueben removed his shoes, whooped for joy as he took off across the marble floor, fell to his bottom and skidded joyfully with his legs in the air. After this show of unbridled joy, I encouraged all my offspring to sit down on the comfortable chairs whilst I checked in. Halfway through the process, I turned around to get the passports from my bag and noticed my children had mounted the sofas and lay like dead tiger skins over the top. I looked back at the receptionist and saw her looking beyond me at my children in the same surprised and disgusted way she would if I had arrived with a herd of feral goats.

As soon as we were in the room, we removed our clothes and let the cool of the air conditioning lick our bodies. Within a few minutes, I was so cold that I wanted a coat and so I climbed into the perfect white sheets despite the mud. I lay there eating cindered peanuts and a complimentary bunch of langan berries. Evan read 'Match of the Day' and Mary lay next to me on the bed. The children quickly discovered the expensive bar fridge loaded with chocolate they could identify. However, the items that caused the most joy were the free slippers and bathrobes. Rueben was delighted with the towelling gown and insisted that we refer to him as 'mini King Solomon'. Carrie came out in her swimming gear and asked that we all go swimming, but Rueben refused unless she paid him due honour. She refused, he relented and then they joined forces in their demand to swim.

After an afternoon in the pool (that we had entirely to ourselves) and a cursory look at the hotel menu that appeared to charge more for a few prawns and rice than the room, we decided to walk down the road in search of more affordable and relaxed places to eat. We found a restaurant that sold live crabs, fish, octopus and opaque crayfish from aerated tanks. It was more to our budget and requirements, with plastic chairs and exposed electrical wiring for the fans that the owners turned on when we sat down. Mary and I were tempted to order fresh seafood but thought we should play it safe and ordered stir-fry. Given our previous encounters with fish murder, I was surprised that Carrie thought the tanks were decorative and so when a family arrived, waved their arms about over the pool, picked a crab, had it weighed and then sat down, she was only intrigued. Five minutes later the crab made an appearance again. This time it lay lifeless on a bed of salad. The locals unsympathetically cracked open the shell and pulled the meat off its back. Carrie was so shocked that she declared she would never eat seafood again.

We walked back in the dark and looked onto the large Bai Chai suspension bridge sitting high over the harbour. At night the bridge was lit up like a disco as it flashed pink, green and yellow, and then flashed like an elaborate neon sign. It was the only pretty thing as we walked back to the hotel. At night, the dust from the construction site made the road look like it was covered in the falling ash of an active volcano.

The following day we hired a boat to tour the world heritage Halong Bay. Whilst the town was ugly, the bay with its one thousand six hundred limestone islands is outstandingly beautiful. For one hundred pounds, we had an entire boat to ourselves with a woman called Dung as our guide. I considered this good value. However, the downside of this cheap deal was that even though we had the boat to ourselves, we were part of a convoy full of Korean and Chinese tourists. Despite the sun being barely above the horizon, the beers and the music on the other boats were already in demand as we chugged across the calm waters of the bay to our first stop. We sat up on the top deck and watched schools of tiny fish leap out of the water.

"Mum", Carrie asked.
"Yes?"
"Why are your arms so hairy?" she asked.

Mary scowled. I yearned for just a second to be on one of the music-blaring, beer-swilling boats.

The convoy stopped at a cave and hundreds of Asians and the Tucker family disembarked. We joined the back of the queue and walked single file into a hole in the cliff whilst piped Vietnamese music floated through the foliage. Guides led enormous groups of bored-looking people along the pathways, declaring interesting facts through microphones and pointing at rock features with green lasers. The cave was large and pretty, and lit with yellows, greens and pinks. However, it was our fellow travellers pulling duckfaces for selfies or posing like Audrey Hepburn that entertained us the most. Evan, Rueben and Carrie were so inspired that they spent much of the time asking me to photograph them whilst they blew kisses at the camera or leant seductively against a stalagmite.

The next part of the tour took us past stunning egg-shaped hills covered in jungle and bursting out of the sea. We stopped by a rock feature in the water that Dung said was named 'Farting Cock' much to the boys' delight. Then she went to the back of the boat and promptly fell asleep. Later that evening, I realised that she meant 'Fighting Cock'. The boys still found this name amusing as well.

We sailed across open water where the only noise was the thudding rhythm of the engine and the plop of candy as the second mate played 'Candy Crush' on his phone. For most of the tour, no one interacted with us. They either slept or played on their phones.

I looked over at the crew and was confused by their disinterest. People paid thousands of pounds to fly to Vietnam to see the bay and yet this crew seemed about as excited about their surroundings as a bored man delivering a sermon. If I was a sailor on Halong Bay, I would fish, enjoy the sea breeze, research the local communities that clung to the islands and look for whales that occasionally visit the brackish waters.

Halong Bay

@@@@@

After Dad died, I was very sad and lonely. I had no girlfriend at the time and, whilst my friends were sympathetic, they did not really understand the dark place where I lived; their parents were still alive. I was desperate for relief and threw myself into anything that dulled the pain. So, when my friend Paul suggested life-modelling as a drunk joke, I needed very little encouragement to do it. I walked to the payphone in the pub, rang the local art college and applied for a job where I would stand naked in front of students. Even though I was a little drunk, I was mostly driven by a reckless desire for attention. After the call, I thought little about it; assuming the college had idiots regularly ringing them up asking for naked work. However, to my surprise, a day later, one of the art tutors called me back and asked me to come to the college for a chat. Within a week I was on the life-model list.

My first few jobs at the college were working with degree students. The first time I was naked, I was made to kneel and stare at an aerial photograph of a local chemical plant and so my bits were hidden. A few times after that though, I stood completely naked for degree classes with nothing hidden; holding artefacts such as a stereo or a rolling pin. In the first few sessions I was so nervous that I ended up counting the bricks in the wall to keep my mind occupied, and always avoided eye contact.

My most regular job though, was sitting for a class for retired people. I spent six months with that group and much of the time we chatted about our lives, loves and struggles. Sitting naked meant that normal social barriers quickly broke down. Often the conversations with the group meandered from painting techniques to things that would not be typically shared. One woman spoke about being gay in 1970s Middlesbrough, one had lost their wife through cancer and saw painting as a healing process and another was a retired priest who loved colours. One day, to my surprise, I stood naked in front of these people who were all broken in their own way and suddenly found my voice to talk about my grief. Looking back, that job was the first step I took in a healing process that took years to complete. I think that if it was not for that job then I may have been too warped to begin falling in love when I met Mary a few months later.

Ever since then, I have always taken jobs where I have been able to show my heart and express myself. Boredom has always made me distressed.

That was why I never understood why Dung and her crew showed such disinterest amid such beauty.

@@@@@

We stopped at an island that had a small beach and advertised cold drinks that in reality were lukewarm. By the time we arrived, the place was full of the Koreans and Chinese, and glum locals. In fact, the only people I saw smiling on that island were Koreans and my children, and that surprised me because the place was beautiful; albeit a little hot.

The two things to do on the island were to swim at a muddy beach and visit a viewpoint. The lookout involved a climb up stairs that Rueben refused to ascend using his own feet. I carried him and the effort in the heat turned me into a soggy mass. Rueben tried to converse with me, but my lungs struggled to get enough wind inside me and so my part of the conversation morphed into painful grunts, but the view at the top was beautiful. I think of that view almost every morning as Carrie had a photograph of us all standing in front of the view and placed it onto a 'World's Greatest Dad' mug that I use for my morning coffee.

We ate on the boat as it chugged back through open waters and ate a delicious dinner of fish cooked in lemongrass, spinach, rice and fish spring rolls. Carrie loved the spring rolls and decided to take a break in her seafood abstinence when she saw the food.

After lunch, Mary and I spoke about tips and decided that (since Dung barely spoke to us and slept for most of the journey) my wallet would stay firmly inside my pocket. However, just as the port appeared on the horizon, Dung became the most animated she had been on the entire trip and managed to persuade Carrie to buy some pearls. Dung demonstrated that they were real by heating them with a lighter to prove they did not melt. Then, Evan and Rueben decided they too wanted a souvenir, and each purchased a necklace. Rueben purchased a cross and it sat a little too large on his chest so that he looked part 'Mr T', part Pope. Soon after we got back to the hotel, Carrie left her pearls too close to a sweet. The sweet melted to the pearl and when she pulled the sweet away, she peeled off a pearl coloured lining and exposed a plastic ball.

Unlike the previous day, we shared the pool in the afternoon with a busload of Koreans. The Koreans only ventured into deeper waters if they sat in a lifesaver they pilfered from the wall. I sat on the poolside keeping a careful eye on my children who played in the deep end; dunking each other. Matters were taken a little too far when Rueben tried to rip Evan's swimmers off, and Evan retaliated by punching Rueben in the testicles; winding him and making him sink. I jumped up, dove into the water and grabbed Rueben from the bottom of the pool. With order restored, I returned to the side and noticed the Koreans hawking out their smoker's phlegm into the drains that lined the pool. I think they thought the water in the drains would not find its way back into the pool. Disgusted, I immediately ordered the children out of the water and made a mental note to avoid public swimming baths if ever I visit Seoul.

After two days in an air-conditioned and marble hotel room, we wanted to see something that felt more like the Vietnam we really liked. Opposite the hotel was a car park that sank into the water of the bay. In the absence of any beach, the locals turned the carpark into the place to hang out of an evening. People sat in plastic chairs, swam in the sea and ate, and so we decided to explore. We dashed across the road to avoid the water-spraying trucks and the banks of wet sand in the gutters, but Carrie mistimed her leap onto the pavement and stepped in one of the banks of mud.

"Yuck! I look like I've just stepped in an ice cream container of poo!" she shouted.

The locals gave us amused stares as we walked into their domain, particularly when Carrie insisted on walking down a cement incline to the water's edge to wash her shoe. None of us realised that close to the water the cement was covered in slime. Carrie suddenly fell. She fell straight onto her bottom and slid towards the bay waters. I ran to rescue her, and I too then hit the slime and started to slide though I stayed on my feet and balanced like I was surfing.

"Mary! Help!" I shouted.

I did not mind getting wet but knew the photos would be ruined if the camera got wet. I looked over my shoulder. Mary stood still; laughing. I glared at Mary.

"Help?" I shouted at her again.

A few seconds later, a local man came and offered me his hand of assistance and I grabbed Carrie. Her mud-covered shoe, however, needed to be rescued from the sea by a small child wearing a life vest.

"Why didn't you come and help?" I spat the words out at Mary.

"Because I was laughing too much," she responded.

I led the family out of the carpark, sulking and stewing, and we trudged along the wall that bordered the construction site for a kilometre until we found a cart selling Bánh Mì.

Bánh Mì is Vietnamese for bread but is often used for a delicious French stick crammed full of barbecued pork and salad covered in chilli sauce. Food always calms our family tensions and the Bánh Mì was no exception.

Feeling far happier and full, we returned to the hotel. The dust choked us, and I was glad to get back to the cool of the hotel; sweaty and coughing. As we approached, Carrie looked up at the hotel signage and laughed. She noticed that the 'ot' on the neon sign on the top of the building was not working and so the hotel advertised itself as Paradise Bay Hel'.

"Sums this place up", she said.

Chapter 5: Hanoi

The bus trip from Halong Bay to Hanoi was uneventful, though a toilet stop at a roadside shop was a source of some excitement for the children. I could have purchased dried fish, chopping boards, a Santa doll, an Eiffel Tower model, a doll in a highland uniform, a chipped vase, a statue of a urinating child, a children's mask of a religious deity and a porcelain cat that looked like it was punching the air; all this was sold from a shop the size of a domestic garage. Driven by boredom, the children wanted me to purchase almost everything listed above, but the only thing I allowed them to buy was a sesame seed bar that was sold to us as a snack. I thought the snack would not have looked out of place hanging from a bird table, but the children enjoyed it.

The distant hills of Halong disappeared over the horizon. Paddy fields littered with electricity pylons and the occasional pocket of tiled gravestones took over the scenery. It was nice to look outside at Vietnamese countryside again after the dirtiness of Halong City, but my attention often drifted to the blaring television that showed the Vietnamese version of the 'X Factor'. Almost every song had a prop like a giant banana or a fake cloud that fell jerkily from the studio roof. We were all drawn in at the beginning of a song wondering what object would fall from the ceiling next, and then sat back and sighed in the hope the next song would be better than the previous one. They never were.

As we neared Hanoi, the scenery began to look more like Halong City again. Everything looked a little dirty. Even a flock of ducks looked like strewn bits of litter on the riverbanks at first. As we drew closer to the city, houses soared above the freeway; some painted lime green and mustard. We passed enormous signs the size of several tennis courts advertising Hanoi beer and one with a confusing message that said, "Produce sagacious power". The road we travelled on crossed high above the river and from my vantage point, I saw incomplete roadways that rose pleasingly into the sky and then stopped; a symbol of the rapid development of this part of the world.

In Hanoi, we checked in to our hotel and then rested until the heat of the day disappeared before venturing out on our first walk. We only walked for thirty seconds around the corner from the hotel and down a road no wider than a double bed before Evan spoke up.

"Dad, I'm hungry", he said in his deep voice the moment we passed a street vendor that sold fresh Bánh Mì full of chilli sauce and fried eggs.

Eating Bánh Mì in Hanoi

We joined the back of a long queue (a sure sign of good and safe street food) and ate the buns as we cowered in the shade created by a colourful graffitied wall that would not have looked out of place in the East End of London.

Conflict resolution at Hoan Kiem lake

With our stomachs filled, we finally stepped out into the city. Hanoi was like nothing else I had experienced before. The only way to cross the road was to step into traffic and assume it would stop, and the only way to walk down many streets and alleys was to share the roads with the cars. Three-storey dwellings magnified the heat onto the road and the people moving around. Balconies shot out of the buildings at chaotic angles; draped in advertising hoardings, flags, sunshades and lanterns. Electricity wires hung like tar-covered spaghetti on poles and looked like they were pinned down by loud speakers. The walk along the alleyways left us overwhelmed and made us walk quickly, as if we were in a hurry to get somewhere even though we had no plans.

Hoping to get some air and feel a sense of space, we made our way to Hoan Kiem Lake and walked over a pretty bridge to a temple. As soon as we arrived, Evan tried to push Rueben into the lake. Rueben threw a tantrum and Carrie refused to look inside any of the temple buildings. The claustrophobia, the heat and the noise took its toll on us all. Mary took the opportunity to photograph my conflict resolution in action.

Hanoi and its amazing electrical wiring

It sounds like we disliked Hanoi but that was not the case. Carrie, Rueben, Evan and Mary's eyes glazed over at the volume of shops selling souvenirs. We went into several shops in the pursuit of purchasing something and came out with a teddy bear wearing a traditional Vietnamese hat and a pile of sew-on badges of all the countries the children visited around the world.

"So, are we done shopping for the day?" I asked as we left.

Everyone looked at me as if I had suggested we all take drugs.

"You can wait outside with Rueben if you like," Mary responded.

Despite the concentration of people and buildings, Hanoi had many avenues full of trees and, whilst the children and Mary shopped, I was content to watch people pass by on bicycles carrying anything from balloons to pans. However, the greatest pleasure I got in the heat and the chaos as I stood outside shops was in looking up at the ancient and gnarled trees and watching the wind flutter in the leaves.

Crossing a road in Hanoi

The trees in Hanoi are something that locals also love. In 2015, a local mother named Duong Ngoc Tra set up a Facebook page to oppose the felling of the trees and she gathered over fifty thousand likes. Her protest gathered so much momentum that the authorities backed down; a rare occurrence in a country that has been ruled by a single party for forty years.

That evening we ate at a restaurant near the cathedral. In the distance, we heard the congregation sing mass. The song sounded as rousing as the South African national anthem. Closer to us, drivers punched at their car horns followed by a sound like a sledgehammer on a metal rivet as their cars went over a temporary ramp. We ate Bun Cha (seared pork, vermicelli noodles and vegetables soaked in a fish soup) in a room with dirty lime-green walls spattered with grease. An electric plug with exposed wiring and a cable that looked like it came from a 1960s television set hung inches from my elbow as I ate. The oily floor indicated the place may have once been a garage, and the air was blue and smoky from the constantly frying meat. We ate and soaked up the atmosphere and perspired. Evan attempted to eat his noodles with a chopstick in each hand and Rueben tore at his noodles as if it were playdough.

"Next time we'll pack some forks," Mary said dreamily looking over her sons.

Watching children eat with chopsticks was amusing but they rarely left dinner feeling full.

I could have sat for far longer and watched Hanoi move around me. However, Rueben suddenly held his hand to his bottom.

"Poo!" he shouted.

We knew it was urgent. Mary grabbed Rueben and Carrie and rushed back to the hotel to get him to the toilet whilst I paid up. The journey back to the hotel seemed far harder than when we made our way to the restaurant because the mass was over and the congregation from the church sat in the alleyways on small plastic chairs eating noodles. In the distance, I heard Rueben give agonised yelps and saw him clench his thighs, but he got to the hotel just in time.

@@@@@

The next morning, we queued for two hours in the sunshine to have the brief pleasure of wandering by four white-clothed soldiers, a stone engraving of the hammer and sickle and the preserved and waxy body of Ho Chi Minh. The volumes of people who wanted to have this experience astounded me that morning. Ho Chi Minh died over half a century before. However, the scores of buses dropping off people to pay homage was a testament to how revered the man is in the country. The mausoleum was not open when we arrived, and we thought getting there early meant the queues would be short. After the taxi dropped us off, however, we walked around a kilometre to the back of the column of people. Each time I thought we came to the end, I realised it was just a break in the line at a road intersection. We walked three blocks of patient and smiling people before we came to the end. At first, I wondered why the place was only open until ten thirty in the morning given its popularity. However, within thirty minutes it was obvious why; standing in the sweat and heat for many hours would not be safe even for the most acclimatised local.

It was so hot; most locals had either paper or battery-operated fans, and a small cottage industry made large sums of money selling bottled water and coke to the waiting crowds. Carrie, Evan and Rueben scowled when they realised the wait in front of them and copious bribes of cold drinks at the hotel were required to stave off a revolt. Just as the queue entered the grounds to go into the mausoleum, Carrie placed her hand on her stomach and bent over. She was in pain. After an hour and being so close to seeing the body, I offered words of encouragement about how close we were to seeing a dead person and that soon she could drink a nice cold coke. However, the effects of these words lasted only a few minutes and it was apparent that she would not last without going to the toilet. I lifted her out of the queue and across a barrier; an activity that alerted the security guards.

"Nar Vey Sin?" I asked uncertainly.

I was not confident on my pronunciation in Vietnamese. Even though I learnt some Vietnamese vocabulary before we came, I quickly realised the pronunciation of a word was everything. For example, if I walked into a restaurant and wanted rice noodle soup, then I would ask for 'pho', but if my pronunciation was subtly wrong then instead of a soup, I would be asking for a prostitute. Fortunately, the guard either understood my question or recognised what Carrie required. He pointed us to a shed that was a few thousand people ahead of us in the queue.

The shed smelt as if something very sweaty had recently died inside. I glanced over at Carrie who amazingly did not flinch as she stepped forward. As I waited outside, a mother and toddler approached. They looked into the darkened door and then stopped. The mother said something to the toddler who pulled down their shorts and simply urinated on the doorstep. Carrie appeared a minute later and looked like she had been disembowelled.

"Never again," she muttered. However, she was empty enough for us to see Ho Chi Minh.

I felt uncomfortable viewing a famous man lying in state. I felt a little like I should not be there, as if I had just entered his bedroom and he was sleeping or that I had stumbled into the wake of a stranger. Surprisingly, though, the locals around us looked on at their former leader with only mild curiosity. I thought there would be some greater emotions shown given the volume of people and the effort they went to, to spend those few seconds filing passed their most famous leader.

"Dad was he dead?" Rueben asked as we left the building.

"Yes. He has been dead for almost the same amount of years that he lived." I responded.

"Huh, he didn't look very scary. When you or Mum die, I think you would look scary," Rueben remarked.

After we viewed Ho Chi Minh's body, we followed the crowds in the hope of finding an exit. However, we saw no sign of escape, and ended up walking by Ho Chi Minh's wooden house and by a garage labelled "Ho Chi Minh used cars". Eventually we found our way out after walking along an avenue lined with shops selling Ho Chi Minh plates, ash trays, busts and posters, and we took a taxi back to the hotel where we sat and watched television, drank coke and Carrie had unfettered access to a clean toilet.

After a rest we had iced coffees in a cafe. We sat on stools that were so low, they were hardly worth bothering with. I noticed that even our drink bottle stood higher than the seats. The coffee, however, was black, sweet and ice cold – it was refreshing and delicious.

We were protected from the sun by a wicker blind that swayed gently in the wind. Two other families sat close by. One family drank iced tea and the other chewed on sunflower seeds. Rueben played with his ice with another child; pretending that the holes in the ice were a necklace when they were threaded onto a drinking straw.

Suitably refreshed, we took a taxi to Hoa Lo road. The building that the taxi driver pointed to was not what I expected. High-rise hotels and electronic shops towered over the place. The front of the building looked colonial and becoming with the words 'Maison Centrale' carved into stone on an arch above the entrance. I took it to mean literally 'Central House' in my terrible understanding of French, but the translation of these two words is 'prison'. It was built by the French to accommodate the Vietnamese who were unhappy about the French occupation. However, when the French left, the Vietnamese recycled the building to house captured US airmen in the Vietnam War and was known by the US prisoners as Hanoi Hilton.

The building was now a museum and gave details of life inside through exhibits and panels. One panel had a black and white photo of a decapitated head and told a story about a small but determined resistance group who in 1908 hatched a plot to kill off the French garrison in Hanoi. The group poisoned the garrison by mixing the pulp of a Datura plant into the meal. The Datura plant has a friendly name of the Moonflower because the flowers smell stronger at night and is known to give colourful dreams and long sleeps to the sniffer. However, ingestion of the plant can be fatal; though a little luck and the right growing conditions are required to provide guaranteed results. In this case, the toxin from the plant they mixed into the food had a kick but was not quite good enough. The cooks managed to make the entire garrison fall into a deep sleep, but none of them died. At this point one of the cooks felt guilty and confessed to a priest, who duly reported the sin to the authorities. Once awake, the French rounded up the perpetrators, housed them in the prison and then sent them to the guillotine. The French then photographed the results of this punishment primarily to dissuade other locals from doing them harm, but also (unintentionally) providing photographic evidence of their cruelty and an exhibit for the museum over a century later.

Most colonial powers did not have great human rights records, but the French in Vietnam may have pipped others in their race to dish out abuse. Cells were designed for maximum discomfort with prisoners tethered to floors that slanted backward so that blood ran to the captive's head. With movement restricted by the tether, the prisoners crapped and ate in the same spot. The French built the place so securely that they proclaimed, "Not even an ant could escape!"

This was clearly propaganda, because in the next room was an exhibition about a group of Vietnamese rebels who escaped the prison one Christmas Eve by crawling through a sewer.

As Mary explained the story to Evan, he sighed, looked up at Mary and asked, "Did they escape so that they could have their Christmas dinner?"

We took a taxi to Bach Ma Temple in the old quarter. It is the oldest temple in Hanoi and arguably one of the smallest. When we first arrived, the taxi driver pointed out the building but I thought he pointed down an alleyway and so I duly led the family into a dark gap between the buildings. After a minute, we turned back when we realised that we had just walked into someone's backyard. The temple was next to the alley and easily missed as it was coloured mustard yellow like many buildings around it and was hidden by a maze of electrical cables. It reminded me of an old colonial house and stepping into the temple was like stepping into a calm oasis from the noise outside.

A kind old woman put on a fan and allowed us to sit down whilst we looked at our maps. Once cooled, we explored the very small but colourful and slightly surreal temple. By standing still and reaching out with my arms, I could touch pyramid shaped incense mounds, a life size wooden horse, a bowl of fruit and a pyramid of golden Hanoi beer cans.

We walked down Mae May street to Memorial House. The house was once a merchant's property but was restored and turned into a museum. We wandered through the lovely old honeycomb-coloured house with dark teak flooring and old 1920s electric fans that provided a delicious breeze. Outside an army of grinning cycle rickshaw drivers waited. Inside we felt exhausted and hot and sat at a table underneath one of the ancient fans. I looked at the map.

"It's about two kilometres back to the hotel Mary. What do you think?"

I am usually a little miserly when it comes to spending money on transport for tourists but carrying Rueben back to the hotel seemed as appealing as discovering a threadworm infestation in my gut. Rueben sat with his head in his hands and did not move and Carrie complained she felt a little weak. I needed to negotiate with the rickshaw drivers. As soon as they saw me, they waved and smiled.

"How much to the cathedral?" I asked

"One hundred and twenty dong"

I paused "Too much. How about twenty?"

The drivers laughed. I laughed back. I knew my starting point was a joke.

"One hundred dong"

"Thirty dong", I responded.

"One hundred dong."

"Fifty dong", I said.

"One hundred dong"

"OK" I turned to walk away and took a few steps down the street.

The family looked at me with hurt alarm; unbelieving that they were to walk across the old quarter to the hotel. Rueben looked like he was about to cry.

"OK fifty dong!" They shouted.

We climbed in though the driver did not look happy.

"No local pay less seventy dong," he grumbled

I pointed out that I have yet to see a single

Vietnamese in a cycle rickshaw. He did not respond.

We returned to the hotel and watched Discovery Channel. Carrie and Evan seemed particularly taken by a program about a man who built pools and managed to create tension in the program by misplacing a rock.

On the final night in Hanoi we went to the markets. It rained just before we headed out and the air was so humid, my underpants felt like a nappy. Carrie stormed ahead of us; ecstatic about the shopping potential. We could buy football shirts, jeans, doughnuts, hairbrushes, schoolbags, naughty underpants, balloons, teapots, smartphone cases and slippers with a scantily-clad image of Britney Spears printed over the big toe. There was even a street we walked down that was dedicated to parties, with each stall and shop stuffed full of balloons, flashing red lights, tinsels and papier-mâché dragons. All the vendors looked tired and bored, but the stalls were very pretty.

@@@@@

In the morning, the children and Mary seemed as enthused about going to the Temple of Literature as they would be about wearing woollen suits in the insufferable heat. The only way they tolerated my request was the fact that after the visit, I promised a trip to Hanoi waterpark.

"Are we done now?" Carrie asked soon after we walked through the temple gate.

Rueben raced over to a fishpond full of scruffy looking lily pads and the occasional fish. A man sat crouching in the shade of a tree overlooking the fishpond looking utterly forlorn and dejected.

"That's exactly how I feel," Carrie muttered to her mother, and gestured towards the man.

I walked past the long rows of tablet-shaped stelae, fenced off from tourists. The children and Mary followed slowly behind. Their heads were bowed, and they looked like every step was an effort, as if they were dragging large cannonballs attached by chains to their ankles. I wandered through an arch with red, blue and white flags fluttering in the breeze that disappointingly did not cool. As I crossed the courtyard towards the main temple, I looked behind and saw the children and Mary give up on the temple and head towards a shop to the side. I carried on walking towards the temple and watched the tourists around me. Everyone looked universally bored. They took photos of the long roof that curved up at the sides and made the main building look like a boat, but spent no time looking at the view. Then they turned around and took another photo of something else. I wondered if they would ever look at the photo again or would look at it and wonder where they took it.

Confucius, his friends and a few storks sat in prime positions in the temple. They all had wispy Ho Chi Minh-style beards (the people not the storks) and all had clothes painted the same red colour as Noddy's car. The statues impressed me, and I thought my family missed out by heading to the shop.

As I walked out of the temple, I saw Rueben throw a minor tantrum at the shop's exit (I think Mary would not allow him to buy anything). I joined the family in the shade and watched my children fight over the last dregs of water. This was not a successful temple visit and I told my offspring that they needed to make a little effort. As a punishment for fighting and not looking at the stelae or temple, I forced them to examine a stela that looked like a gravestone that sat on top of a carved turtle. When we looked closer, the turtle had a delicate and rounded face.

"Hey, look at the face – it looks like a seal!" I tried to cajole them back to some happiness.

"Like I care, Dad," Carrie sighed.

"When are we going to the pool Dad?" Evan asked.

Rueben looked at me and asked, "Why are we

here?"

Mary looked at me and laughed.

If the Temple of Literature had been one of the most tedious experiences the children had in Vietnam, Ho Tay waterpark was probably the most fun if not the most surreal. However, the experience did not begin well. As soon as we left the temple, a taxi driver waved us over and, in our eagerness to get to somewhere more fun, we followed him. We knew the journey was a little out of town and perhaps took twenty minutes, but the meter seemed to be moving far quicker than in any other taxi we took. The fare came in at a cost that was slightly less than the taxi from Ninh Binh to Halong, a journey of nearly four hours. Already in a bad mood for cheating us, the driver did nothing to endear himself to us when he parked up next to a dirty pond full of lily pads and beckoned us to get out. We did not move until he took us the extra kilometre to the entrance.

An orchestral version of 'I will always love you' piped out across a deserted park and was the only sign of life at the park.

"Is this place even open?" Mary asked me with a grimace on her face.

"I hope so. There is no way I'm going back into the centre with that driver," I responded.

A few minutes before, Mary urged me to challenge the driver about his meter, though I refused since I was not sure if having an argument with a taxi driver who knew almost no English would achieve anything. I think she was irritated by my minor cowardice.

We paid our dues and were beckoned through turnstiles that may have been of the correct height for Vietnamese but banged awkwardly on my knees as I passed through. Once inside, the piped electronic music echoed against the adjacent dormant rollercoaster. The avenue from the turnstiles to the park was vast and the only sign of life was a single vendor standing next to a pile of over a thousand multi-coloured glass cups. They grinned at us in the hope that we would purchase one. I thought it an odd thing to sell people going into a swimming pool; a bit like selling beer to people about to walk into a church or livestock outside a posh hotel. It was obvious there were more staff around than paying guests, but the great thing about an empty waterpark was that there were no queues. The children were beside themselves with excitement but that quickly turned into shouts of 'Come on!' and foot stamping in exasperation at their parent's slowness at changing into swimmers, locking away our belongings and slapping sunscreen on them all.

The first ride I took was a covered water tube and let in no light. Hot air blasted my face as I tore down in the darkness. I should have seen the low turnstiles as a warning, but failed to see any danger and entered the plunge pool designed for people far smaller than I. I flew across the plunge pool, smashed into a serrated tile at the edge and gave myself a large cut to my wrist from which I still carry a scar.

Mary and I took turns looking after Rueben, who spent much of his time in the pool called "The four-year-old pool". It had a life-size Asian elephant, three slides and a strange concrete pumpkin covered in mould that spat water right at my crotch whenever I passed by. It hurt when it hit its target, but after a few painful experiences, I learnt to pass the pumpkin with due caution.

As we left, we passed the seller with her armada of glass cups. With almost no punters, she gave up with sales and was busy cleaning every single one. She looked miserable, which was a shame because we had a fantastic time.

That evening, we took a taxi to the train station. According to my map, the journey was only a few blocks away. I suspected that we were going in the wrong direction after ten minutes, and my suspicions grew as the driver took a turn that looked like it led to a four-lane highway. For the second time, a taxi driver saw our luggage and thought we wanted the airport. This time, Mary was not required to do her train impressions and I simply pulled out the tickets.

Because of this error, we passed by the Ho Chi Minh mausoleum where we saw the Vietnamese leader lying in state the previous day. Seeing the building from a distance made me realise the scale of place. It was enormous. The floor to ceiling red banners on the outside looked like giant ribbons.

"Dad, that building looks like a present." Evan observed.

I agreed with him. I also noticed the guards that stood inert outside the entrances to the mausoleum. Dressed all in white, they looked like cruise ship staff with automatic rifles.

Chapter 6: Dong Hoi and Paradise Cave

That evening we took the SE99 train from Hanoi to Dong Hoi and arrived at six thirty-five in the morning. Again, I remembered the reviews of Vietnamese trains that described the system as being old, in need of investment and often late. However, again, my experience of Vietnam trains is that they were great. Our train from Hanoi left exactly on time and arrived many hours later at Dong Hoi station a hundred miles away. It was just three minutes late.

Our hosts at the guesthouse in Dong Hoi smiled as they greeted us even though we arrived at seven o'clock in the morning; seven hours before our booked time. I immediately liked the hotel. It had a fishpond underneath the stairs in the foyer where most hotels kept brooms or fax machines, a statue of a naked woman draped in just a towel in an alcove and a statue of Confucius against a pillar near the front door. All around was dark poo coloured furniture.

Even though we had no rights to a room, the hosts gave us a breakfast of Vietnamese sausage, eggs (fried) and a soft baguette. We ate outside at a table on the pavement and enjoyed the cool morning breeze. It should have been idyllic, but the pace of travelling had begun to take its toll on us. Carrie and I temporarily lost any sense of perspective and had a robust debate about whether she should eat her hard-boiled yoke. I won, but only under the threat of having coke taken away from her for a day. To make matters worse, we had to swat away black midges as we ate. Whenever they landed on us (which was a lot of the time) they itched and left us irritable.

Understandably, our room was not ready that early in the morning and so we showered in a shared shower. All the males in the family took a communal decision; that we will wear no underpants for the entire day. It was a great decision. Still, the only clean t-shirt in my possession had a hole round the collar that left me liable to get a burn on my neck the shape of triangle. Mary thought the t-shirt made me look homeless.

@@@@@

I often think that every corner of the world has been explored, at least those corners that do not require humans to wear diving suits or breathing apparatus. Whilst new discoveries are getting rarer, sometimes a place is discovered that evokes the golden days of discovery when Cook discovered Australia or Darwin toured the world on HMS Beagle. In 1995, a local man led some British cavers to a gash in a rock halfway up a mountain in the jungle near Dong Hoi. It did not look like much, but the small entrance led to a cave. The cave went back over thirty-one kilometres with a floor to ceiling height over one hundred metres in some places. Then in 2009, another cave (Hang Song Doon) was found nearby with dimensions that made it the largest on earth.

A few years after the discovery, the Vietnamese authorities created stairs and access to the Paradise Cave and charged tourists a hefty fee to experience one of the largest natural caverns in the world. I find it life-affirming that such discoveries are still made in modern times - even in populous regions of the world like Vietnam.

We hired a middle-aged driver who spoke no English but smiled a lot and seemed happy to serve us. He drove us towards a distant line of mountains and past fields of rice and cassava. In the cool of an air-conditioned car and along the best maintained roads we experienced in Vietnam, the journey was highly agreeable for me. No one else in the family saw anything; they slept in the back after a night on a train.

It took around an hour to drive to an enormous car park in the middle of the jungle. Judging by its size, the authorities expected a lot of footfall at the cave, though when we arrived there were ten other cars parked up on the new asphalt. We paid about fifty pounds to enter the cave. Even after the fee, they wanted to charge for a golf cart ride to the foot of the hill. It was something we refused but lived to regret as we sweated below thick jungle foliage. Still, the butterflies that fluttered around kept us entertained. Finally, we came to the foot of a hill that rose sharply. This was as far as the golf buggy could have got us. We were welcomed with the sign "Cave Entrance – 570 metres" but we were a soggy mess and five hundred and seventy metres up a hill felt as if we were to undergo a marathon having just run one. We all felt like we wanted to burst into tears. The path climbed in hair pin bends up the steep hill. I carried Rueben and was drenched.

The cave entrance was just a small gap between rocks. We climbed down into a magnificent cool cavern and, at the bottom, the pathway continued for a kilometre. Vast orange-lit cauliflower stalagmites and stalactites rose above us or dropped from the roof. Throughout most of the cave, five-storey houses could easily be built. Despite its awesome natural scale, the stairs meant that anyone could access the cave including a gang of rowdy Vietnamese men screaming, yelping and smoking bongs. Having said that, I was fortunate at one point to be alone with only an enormous phallic-shaped stalactite for company. The silence was absolute, and the cool temperature was splendid.

Walking out into the jungle and onto the vast hot

concrete carpark, the temperature felt like it rose by ten degrees. I was certain that it was the hottest place on earth. There were no other tourists around and so we were the sole focus of an army of over-excited stall holders who waved at us. "You! Come!" and "Hey You!" they shouted. Mary refused to spend money with people who shouted at us and so objected when I was about to spend the equivalent of sixty pence on some small sesame seed toffees and a bottle of water. Evan sat against the post and looked like he was about to cry, Rueben could not refrain and burst into tears and Carrie screamed for water. Just as we were to give in to the children's demands, our friendly taxi driver appeared, and Mary fulfilled her desire not to do any business with people who scream.

However, this unsatisfactory situation was about to get worse.

We decided to eat as soon as we arrived at a nearby local beauty spot to satisfy the children's hunger and thirst. It was only a few minutes away from the cave and seemed a lot less intense than the sellers at the carpark and so, at first, we were all pleased with Mary's choice. We drank cold cokes and sat on a suspended platform looking over the river. I needed to be careful how I sat on my chair, for the back legs wobbled and if they broke then I would be tipped head first onto the rocks below. We ordered food, and even though we were hungry, we tried to appreciate our surroundings of limestone karsts, jungle foliage and the river.

After thirty minutes there was still no food. Evan grimaced and scowled and looked like he was in great pain. This was how he often showed his hunger. There was still no food after forty-five minutes and even our driver became a little irritated. He walked over to the kitchen area and I assume he enquired about the length of time it was taking for our food to be delivered since he pointed at our table. Evan and Rueben were chewing the straws that sat in the empty coke bottles. We waited over an hour before a few paltry dishes arrived.

After the delays, I was in no mood to pay extra money to swim in the river, but to eat and then move on and not have a cooling swim seemed even more unappetising. I therefore paid the entrance fee to walk around fifty metres to get to a swimming hole.

The trail was some bamboo platforms that took us one hundred meters along the roadside to a swimming hole. It was hardly inspirational, but the water was refreshing and cool and tinted a chemically-enhanced blue from the limestone. We all needed to wear lifejackets (an extra cost even though we paid a considerable entrance fee). One of the men giving us the jackets tried to squeeze Rueben as if he were testing for ripeness and made Ruben stumble back and cut his foot. Mary and I were silently furious as our son's screams silenced the jungle birds and made the picnicking locals laugh. Getting into the water was also an exercise and involved me lowering myself from a low bridge into the water and then Mary handing Rueben to me. The ensuing screams of shock from Rueben as his body was immersed in cold waters was far greater than before when he cut his foot.

I swam with Rueben for a few minutes and then slightly longer with Carrie and Evan. The river was fast moving and with a sizeable cascade that had bone breaking potential just twenty metres away, it was not relaxing, but it was great fun and the best part of the beauty spot.

That evening we lay on the bed in the hotel, sporting headaches. My output into the toilet bowl was the colour of dark ale and I suspected I was dehydrated, but the hypochondriac in me wondered if this was the beginning of a bout of cerebral malaria. I lay on the bed and tried to rest, Mary read the 'Rough Guide to Vietnam' on the top bunk, Evan and Carrie watched their favourite program about people who make swimming pools and Rueben watched the Disney channel. I watched Rueben for several minutes; his mouth was open, and a crisp sat half in and half out of his mouth. I think he forgot it was there.

As the afternoon became evening, we walked to an old bombed-out church that sat on the waterfront. It was a famous landmark in Dong Hoi and served as a war memorial. If it was not for this ruined reminder, it would be difficult to see any sign of the conflict, because the seafront looked idyllic. The locals rigged up hammocks in the shade nearby and a fleet of fishing boats painted red, blue, peppermint green and white bobbed gently on the harbour. All the boats proudly flew the Vietnamese flag. As we walked along the promenade, groups of speed-walking women approached us from the opposite direction. They stopped to touch and hail Rueben with joyful staccato-sounding words. He responded with a scowl and a wave of fist; an action that made the women laugh and try even harder to stroke his cheek or rub his belly.

Further along the front, we watched fishermen in their coracles, fishing using enormous nets that were rigged up like upturned umbrellas. They lowered the net into the water for a few minutes and then pulled it up using rigging and gears. Once it was a few feet above the water, they rowed out wearing plastic sombreros to empty the nets through a hole in the centre of the net. We sat as a family on some steps for half an hour and watched them fish. To be outside enjoying the climate but not feeling sweaty left us all smiling. Even the boys sat still for a few minutes. The fishermen's ramshackle huts built on stilts in the sea looked romantic but judging by the fact that I did not see them catch a fish, I suspected they saw their lives in another way.

For dinner, we ate prawn pancakes, salad and various unidentified vegetables wrapped in rice paper and dipped in a tangy fish sauce. The motherly cook spoke no English, but she smiled and spoke with us happily as if we understood every word and showed us how to roll the local delicacy.

On our return to the hotel, we passed another disco-lit bridge. Canoodling teenage couples sitting at a park bench suddenly separated as they became aware of our presence just before we passed by. I do not think they were there just to enjoy the cool evening breeze and the illuminated bridge.

I liked Dong Hoi and was sad that we needed to leave the following morning. However, at daybreak, Mary woke up covered in itchy lumps on her arms and legs. I pulled back her pillow to see tiny red dots. I immediately knew what I was looking at after a similar experience with Mary years before in Malaysia. Overnight, an army of bedbugs had feasted on her flesh. They were so drunk on her blood that they were barely able to hop off into hiding. It was a shame our time in Dong Hoi finished that way because every time I talk with Mary about the town, she starts scratching at her arms and legs.

Chapter 7: Hue

On the final night of January 1968, a single flare shot into the sky and heralded one of the most famous battles between the US and North Vietnamese. Even though the US won the battle, some say that it cost them the war. The attack happened during the national Tet holidays and coincided with attacks across South Vietnam.

Just before the flare was launched, the North Vietnamese took the upper hand as they gained access to the citadel; the fortified old town of Hue. They did this by a few of them dressing up in South Vietnamese army fatigues, walking up to the guards on sentry duty, killing them and opening the gates for their compatriots to enter. Battalions of North Vietnamese streamed into the citadel and drove straight to the north corner where a garrison of South Vietnamese soldiers had their headquarters. By eight o'clock in the morning, the North Vietnamese flag flew from the citadel, but the South Vietnamese garrison held their position and with the support of other South Vietnamese battalions, defended their headquarters for a month.

Sixteen kilometres south of Hue, American forces were attacked but also stood their ground. Americans soon began to push into Hue to repel the North Vietnamese. However, unlike other engagements as part of the Tet offensive that lasted around a week, the battle for Hue went on for four times longer and involved house-to-house combat. Whilst the US forces were in the clear ascendancy, the North Vietnamese used snipers and booby traps to defend their ground. The US forces, who promised never to bomb the city, found battle conditions so challenging that they changed their minds. By the time the North Vietnamese left, seventy percent of all buildings, including those in the citadel, were turned to rubble and over one thousand people were dead. US and South Vietnamese forces claimed victory, but the timing of the battle coincided with the decline in public support for the war in the US.

@@@@@

When we arrived over eighteen thousand days later, the battle scars were covered. Our train into Hue arrived mid-morning and to avoid the heat of the day we relaxed by the small pool in the guesthouse. The sign by the pool said 'Light Garde' hotel. I am not certain what happened to the 'n', but Rueben told us that he suspected it fell into the pool and was swallowed by a guest with a tattoo. When we arrived, there were people lounging all around the pool in a small courtyard, but within five minutes, they were all gone. Possibly this was because the children designed a new jump called "Jonah and the Whale" which involved displacing as much water as possible.

As I sat by the pool, I looked at the time we had left and compared it to what we wanted to see. I realised that if we were to see the citadel, then we needed to go that afternoon. Knowing how fatigued the family all were, I felt as inclined to go as I would if I needed to see a dentist on Christmas Day.

"Come on everyone, we need to go since we may never come here again," I told the family, though really this was a message for me.

"Why do I need to go Dad?" Evan asked.

I half ignored his question, but also did not respond because I was too tired to think of an answer.

Getting everyone ready that afternoon felt more of a duty than a pleasure and I needed to clap my hands and shout to get my children and wife to leave the hotel.

We entered through the main gateway and immediately Rueben and Evan's interest grew, which was good because I had no inspiration or spare energy to get them excited. The gateway, with its oriental roof and yellow and red striped walls, looked like the palace from a children's favourite kung foo film and the boys jumped out of the taxi and ran to the entrance; eager to explore. They became even more animated after we entered because on both sides of the palace were two fishponds. I do not know what they put in the water in these fishponds, but the volume and size of the goldfish were unnatural. Rueben threw some food in and howled in delight at the ensuing scrum of a thousand goldfish that churned the water and made it look like it was boiling furiously.

Rueben running to see the fish at Hue citadel

After the initial excitement, our legs soon felt heavy from a fug of tiredness. We walked through temples and crossed wide paved courtyards the size of several football pitches and past grass knolls where the grass was a bit long and unkempt; it looked like landfill. There were huge ornamental gates covered in peeling paint that sat in fields. The gates may have led to somewhere once but now stood alone and we were too tired and disinterested to work out their purpose. We walked along covered walkways in long pavilions with lacquered timbered rooves and walls obviously restored, for the paintwork shone as if it went on only a few weeks before.

In one of the pavilions, we came across a Vietnamese family having their photograph taken in what we guessed were royal garments, but they made them look like an Asian version of the Beatles on the Sergeant Pepper album. The children and I could not supress our giggles at how ridiculous they looked. The father did not smile as the photographer took the shots and at one point stormed down the stairs in his fluffy pirate hat. I thought we were about to be chastised for laughing. However, he looked at the images just taken and stormed back up whilst barking something at the photographer. His annoyance was not because he was embarrassed but more because the photographer was not portraying him in the correct sanctimonious light that he desired.

I quietly swore as I reached the main entrance at the end of our visit and immediately realised that our planned exit was closed. They locked it up just five minutes before we returned. To make matters worse, monsoon rain pelted us and lightning fizzed overhead. After one burst, Evan broke down; terrified that he would die by lightning. He cowered and shook in the corner of the gate. Rueben grabbed his crotch and looked at me in alarm. Clearly, we could not leave by the way we came and after a consultation of the map, I saw that we needed to run to a distant side exit. We were instantly soaked the moment we started to run, and Evan howled as if he were running a steeplechase with burst haemorrhoids. In his mind, he thought he was sprinting for his life and gripped my hand so hard that it left a bruise.

The excursion had not gone to plan, but it was not the citadel's fault. Looking back, I was pushing the family too hard.

We changed at the hotel and waited for the rains to stop. That evening we ate at a street stall run by a woman called Hong. She looked tired but had an amazing smile as she added chilli, salt, pepper, caramelised onions, herbs and cooked duck into bowls. The dish was called Xoi Ga and was delicious. When our host had no customers, she sat with us and marvelled that we had three children. Rueben charmed her by shovelling rice into his mouth and showing her the contents.

The next day, we ate breakfast at a table that was next to a shelf with an enormous statue of two mating pigs surrounded by tulips. The children and I laughed at the sight of the beasts, but Mary just winced. She was in agony over the hundreds of tiny bites that covered her body from her night in Dong Hoi.

"So, what are we doing today Dad?" Carrie asked.

When I told Carrie that we were to take a trip along the Perfume River to see some tombs, she looked at me and scowled. Her brothers quickly followed. The atmosphere turned from laughter over copulating pigs, to despondency.

"I can't believe you are going to take us away from the pool to look at old things again," Carrie whined as she put her head into her hands.

There was nothing I could do as I had paid for the tour in advance.

After breakfast, we met a young man called Tam who told me he was the captain of our cruise boat and was born on the river. At the beginning of the holiday, this would have been nice to hear, but having travelled for the last week with no more than two nights sleep in the same hotel, I felt tired of such tales.

"Whatever," I thought.

Tam told us we would travel on a dragon boat. However, in the mood I was in, to me the boat looked more like a long aluminium dinghy with a tin dragon template stapled to the helm. He then tried to sell us lunch as soon as we boarded but we refused; thinking and hoping we would be back by midday.

The boat had worn and weathered floorboards that had turned smooth with decades of wear, and linoleum that reminded me of the flooring in my kitchen when I was a child. Tam started the motor with an energetic turn of the crank. We kicked off our shoes and felt the warm boards on the soles of our feet. It was one of the few pleasant sensations I remember of the morning. As we chugged up the Perfume River, we passed cargo boats that carried huge mounds of fine sand. Their load was so heavy, the bow and stern of the boats sat just above the waterline. A few similar dragon boats passed us. I suspect we were travelling on the slowest tourist boat that day. On the shore, women washed clothes and ancient boats squatted against the bank, firmly moored. The hulks looked like rotting carcasses but the fact they were moored suggested they were still in use.

Carrie wanted to sleep, and Mary stared at the horizon; concentrating on anything but the severe itching caused by the bed bugs at Dong Hoi. The boys sat in silence and to an outsider we looked miserable, as if there was an ongoing family argument. Tam tried to cheer us up by offering to take Evan for a swim (it did not happen) and showed me comments on his phone from Swedish people who praised his amazing captaincy. He even gave Evan a t-shirt.

"Now you need to take motorbike to tomb," he told me, smiling.

An extra cost for motorbikes was not part of the deal and I gritted my teeth and fought hard not to complain. I quickly lost the battle and opened my mouth, but to my surprise and (in retrospect) relief, Evan interrupted.

"Carrie guess what! We get to ride motorbikes again! Can you remember in Sri Lanka when we rode them?" he shouted.

There was no way I could complain now.

Our captain moored by what looked like a poorly maintained dirt track and a waterway. At the top of the muddy path, three resting men suddenly got up at the sight of us and ran to get their bikes whilst their wives tried to sell us water, coke or beer from trays they hastily made up for us. I did not want to pay for motorbikes and did not want to purchase drinks even though the children looked at me and pleaded. As we had no choice in transport to the tombs, I had no negotiating power and so was relieved when their quote seemed surprisingly fair.

Rueben travelled with me, Mary travelled by herself and Carrie and Evan travelled together on a bike (we all had drivers as well). Strangely, they had helmets for everyone except Rueben, whose head was too small.

We sent chickens flying as we zoomed up and down backroads and shortcuts between the tombs. I had Rueben sandwiched firmly between the rider and myself, with my arms hugging the rider in front and securing my youngest boy. I knew I was invading all personal bubbles though I saw it as a necessary precaution to ensure Rueben did not come off the bike and end up like the man we saw in Danang. We arrived minutes before everyone else and I had visions of spending the rest of my life with only Rueben for company as I stood and waited nervously looking up the hill. Suddenly a bike roared over the crest carrying Carrie and Evan. They sported huge grins and were clearly focused on the thrill and fun of travelling on motorbikes across Vietnamese countryside rather than any potential brain traumas.

The first tomb we visited belonged to Khai Dinh. This man was a king for ten years at the turn of the twentieth century and seems about as liked by the Vietnamese as enemas. He was a king who submitted happily to French rule and spent a fortune on a grand trip to France for a fair and increased the tax his subjects paid to finance the building of his tomb. He gambled, took drugs and preferred the company of his burly bodyguard at night rather than his wife. When he died at the age of forty, it appears he did nothing in his ten-year reign to ingratiate himself to his people. However, the king had a funeral that included elephants, sumptuous gold pillars, marching bands and a mausoleum that still stands proud above the Perfume River.

The mausoleum sat high above the road and we had to climb steep steps to the entrance. Carrie expended lots of energy as she huffed and stomped to communicate to us all what she thought about ascending stairs in thirty-five-degree heat, and Rueben showed outright defiance by walking in front of me and then stopping so that I would pick him up and put him on my shoulders. We wandered past figures that looked like the Xian Terracotta Army in China, only these statues were granite and were a little over a century old. Inside the mausoleum were pictures of a young king with pomaded hair that gave it the shape of a bread loaf but the colour of coal. He reminded me of a science fiction baddie.

The ceramic mosaics of the tombs were stunning. There were bulging eyes on the dragons, flowers in vases, walking sticks with oriental handles and, confusingly, a bird that had fallen off its perch with another one looking on in alarm. Rueben refused to walk down the stairs and it took some amazingly gentle mothering and a promise of more riding on the motorbike to get him back to street level.

We got on the bikes again and went to Mausoleum number two; the Mausoleum of Tu Doc. Tu Doc was an emperor who lived fifty years before Khai Dinh and, due to a bout of smallpox, this king fired blanks. Still, he did not let that interfere with his love life and married one hundred and four women and kept a harem for emergencies. His mausoleum with a pavilion next to a lake was supposed to be beautiful but when we visited, the lake was drained, and scaffolding lay everywhere. It took around five minutes to look around the building site and then we left. The only comment I remember was when Rueben noticed a cage with a stick in it.

He stared at it for some time and then asked "Dad, why is the stick in the cage? Is it dangerous?"

We paid our drivers and took the boat again. The journeys on the motorbikes made everyone feel more awake and in a better mood and so we purchased cold drinks, watched the jungle and rifled through the tatty souvenirs on Tam's boat that had faded and dog-eared with age. However, the good feeling we had always felt a little transient and I knew the children and Mary could soon revolt.

I think the final tomb we visited (the tomb of Emperor Minh Manh) was stunning and to my surprise and relief, we remained happy. We got off the boat and walked up a dirt path with bamboo growing all around us, showed our guard the ticket and wandered around the complex in almost complete solitude. Compared to the previous two mausoleums, this tomb was on a huge scale with vast boulevards and symmetrical gardens. Butterflies fluttered around us and tiny birds darted around in the shade. I wanted to spend a long time there and felt envious when I spotted a couple who lounged in a nice spot under the shade of a tree.

Knowing it best to not force my children to engage

with this tomb, I left Carrie and Evan perfecting handstands on the enormous paved courtyards. I knew even Mary was tired of old buildings in Vietnam and that even she would tolerate only a short visit. With all this in my mind, I hurried around with Rueben. In the main tomb, yellow rosettes were tied to ornamental balustrades. It was as if the buildings were dressed-up for a special occasion. With no one around the building felt beautiful, forlorn and empty. To me it felt like the end of a party where most of the people had left. It suddenly dawned on me that the trip was almost over and even though I felt tired, I wanted the good times to roll on. I felt bad that we had all been so miserable on the final day of our Vietnamese adventure.

We got back on the boat and I felt low as we chugged back. I wanted to enjoy the last few minutes of the river but needed to deal with children as they bickered over turns on the hammock. Rueben tried to make things better by sharing his packet of squid-flavoured crisps called 'Ring Rong' with his brother, sister and Dad. They tasted like toffee, chilli and fish all rolled up into a crisp.

@@@@@

Two days later, we were home in the UK. It was the typical cold, grey summer morning that seemed to blight the summer holidays. Carrie continued to provide excellent service to the toilet with her rusty nail water though rather worryingly she had a cough and a mild fever. With time differences, we all woke up at five thirty in the morning desperate for breakfast. I made Mary a cup of tea and returned to bed where we sat and looked at the photos of the holiday. Mentally I never felt better though physically I felt like I just dug up an entire graveyard. All my limbs ached.

Mary took a sip of tea as the rain pattered against

our window.

"I can't believe that the trip really happened," she said as I flicked through the images on a tablet.

She asked where the children were, and I explained that they ate breakfast whilst I made the tea and were now upstairs playing. I took a sip of coffee and scratched my head.

Suddenly Mary jumped back in shock.

"Dave what's that?" Again, she showed her fantastic knack of making statements in the form of a question. She knew exactly what it was.

A small black louse crawled along a hair follicle. When Mary tried to pull it off, it jumped and landed on the pillow. Mary darted out of the bed. The last time she took such a hasty retreat from that place was because I was violently sick on the duvet. She approached me cautiously; squinting. It did not take long for her to discover other small black insects in my hair and around my ears. Further inspection showed that Rueben also carried black insects in his head.

Great memories, photographs, my diary and cheap souvenirs were not the only things I brought back from Vietnam.

CAMBODIA

Angkor Wat

BattamBang

Tonlé Sap

KamPong Chhnang

Phnom Penh

KamPot

Kep

Chapter 1: Siem Reap and Angkor Wat

Mary sat behind me in the aisle seat and so had the easiest access to the bags. I sat in a window seat; cornered-in by Rueben who sat next to me and a Chinese lady who sat in the aisle seat.

"Mary do you mind getting me the passports and a pen please?" I asked.

She looked at me and scowled; irritated that she needed to remove her earphones.

"What?" she snapped.

"I need help with these forms. Can you please pass me the passports and pen from the bag? Please?" I asked with an emphasis on the final word in the hope that politeness would lead to compliance.

"Let's just do it at the airport," she said, dismissively.

"No, I want to do it now so that we can get through customs. You know I hate queueing at customs."

She tutted as she stood up, grabbed the bag, rifled for the required papers and threw them at me.

There were three forms per person that needed completing before we entered Cambodia. I filled out all the forms at my table that was the size of a shoebox. In such a cramped space, the forms regularly fell from the table and ended up by my ankles, requiring a lot of straining to bend down and pick them up. After thirty minutes of form-filling, I realised I had made a mistake on Evan's birthday and needed to do his forms again. My forearm felt tender from over stretching and I began to feel emotional.

"Dad can you unwrap my knife and fork?" Rueben shouted at me shortly after his children's dinner was delivered, unaware of the fact he wore earphones with the volume turned up.

His knife and fork for his meal were packaged up in sealed plastic wrapping so strong they would have survived nuclear winters. My elbow bumped the table and sent a few forms floating to my ankles again. I could not open the packaging with my hands and only when I gripped the wrapping with my teeth did the utensils fly out.

"Thanks Dad."

I turned back to my forms.

"Dad!" Rueben was still shouting.

I inhaled deeply, trying to calm my heartbeat.

"DAD!"

"WHAT!" I responded.

"When we arrive at Siem Reap airport, how far is it to the hotel?"

I closed my eyes and rubbed the bridge of my nose.

"I don't know," I sighed, "I've never been there before."

I continued with the forms.

"DAD", Rueben asked, still shouting.

"When we get there, will the pool still be open?"

"I don't know, though it's unlikely as we will get there at midnight," I spoke the words through gritted teeth, spitting each word out.

I placed the pen down and felt like I too wanted to shout. Part of me wanted to cry.

"DAD!" Rueben shouted, still oblivious of the stress he caused.

I turned to look at him.

"Can I help you with what you are doing?" he asked and smiled at me before snuggling up to my aching arm. His touch soothed me.

@@@@@

The walk into Seam Reap the following morning was always going to feel overwhelming. Our body clocks told us it was two o'clock in the morning as we walked out of the entrance of the hotel and onto a dirt road. The first obstacle we had to navigate was a large three-storey house getting demolished between the hotel and the main road. We heard the large thud as the digger smashed against the concrete above our heads and scarpered onto the other side of the street, tripping over a cable sticking out of the pavement.

We walked along a road that ran parallel to the Tonle Sap River with shops on one side where men sat on the floor, hunched over the spare parts of motorbikes. On the banks of the river, green grass and pond weeds provided homes to piles of bin bags. People stood around on the banks and fished, sitting in the shadow of a tree or a motorbike. Some fishermen did not even bother to remove their bike helmets.

It was difficult to look up and take in the surroundings. All along the footpath, the stones that supported the gutter were gone and so the block paving slipped towards the road and made our path lumpy and treacherous. Cables and exposed metal piping stuck out in random places. If a trip on uneven paths did not injure, being impaled was a reasonable possibility. I held Rueben's hand as it quickly turned sticky from sweat. As we walked and wilted in the humid sunshine, tuk-tuks (in Cambodia these are metal chariots pulled along by motorbikes and called remorks) passed us; slowing down and hailing us, hoping for some business.

By the time we walked a mile into the town centre and to Pub Street, we were covered in the familiar sweat that enveloped the family in Asia.

"Please can we order an iced coffee or something?" Carrie whined and squinted as she looked over at a row of restaurants.

Pub Street appeared to be a road full of pizzerias and tanks full of fish ready to nibble at crusty feet. It was a road set up for Western tastes and it reminded me more of a road in a busy tourist enclave on a Greek holiday island. For my first sojourn out in Cambodia, I hoped for something a little more Asian and had no interest in spending money there.

Mary agreed with me and we ushered the family a block away in the hope of finding something less Western. However, there was no change to the shop fronts. In mine and Mary's malaise, we became incapable of deciding on where we should drink. We walked several kilometres trying to find a place that would sell us an iced coffee, but everything reminded us of anonymous coffee shops in UK shopping centres. As the heat and jet lag took its toll, Rueben fought back tears and Carrie skulked, half-embarrassed and half-exhausted by her parent's indecision. Evan managed to stub a toe and limped along like he had snapped a ligament.

We wandered away from the centre and along roads bordered by empty concrete buildings and gates manned by sleeping security guards. At one point we were forced to move quickly out of the way of a small child riding a bike that was so big for him he could only peddle in the top half of the peddle rotation. Shortly after he passed us, we heard a clutter of metal and saw him struggle for control as he collided against a wall. His misfortune created a little distraction from our search.

Out of desperation, we walked into a local hotel and ordered some cokes and iced coffees (the iced coffee tasted a little like instant coffee made with cold water). Rested and a little refreshed, we decided to search for some snacks and fruit, and noticed a market listed on our map. We set off with renewed hope, but the same dispiriting glass fronted shops morphed into enormous hotels bordered by decorative fish ponds full of dead leaves and soggy litter. After walking several blocks, we gave up searching for a local market and entered a supermarket that was air-conditioned and sold everything wrapped in plastic. It was the Asian equivalent of a seven eleven store.

On the way home, we came across a Buddhist temple complex that our guidebook said was named Wat Preah Prohm Rot. Whilst I will never remember the name without looking at my diary, I will always remember the statue in the courtyard of a man with eyes that bulged out of his head in comic alarm as his innards were eaten by birds. I think I too would have looked alarmed if I had storks perched over me and picking out my guts. Finally, I found something that piqued at least one of my children's interest.

Mary, Carrie and Evan sat on a park bench; squinting in the heat and looking utterly dejected. Rueben and I, however, walked around a courtyard lined with green tiles and looked at stray cats with no tails that turned to us and hissed; ready to attack if we got too close.

Outside we chatted to a remork driver with a gentle face. He introduced himself as Sobeit and we arranged for him to take us to a place to buy some fruit from a market (rambutan and bananas). The novelty of riding in a rickshaw once more, coupled with the welcome breeze caused by our movement left us all happier. On the way back, we passed the demolished house.

"In England they'd have closed the road," Carrie said.

Here a few witches hats were placed on the ground to mark significant lumps of rubble too big to move by hand. The hats seemed to be regarded as fun obstacles by the locals on motorbikes, who raced towards them and swerved around them at the last possible moment.

That afternoon, my mind was like mush and the

safest and most relaxing place was sitting by a pool eating bananas packed with taste and the size and look of a swollen thumb. At around five o'clock in the evening, big dark clouds rolled and within thirty minutes, bucket loads of water fell and smashed against the decorative paving stones outside our hotel room.

After the storm we walked into town and navigated our way around enormous puddles and damp rubbish. Carrie got a few spatters of mud on her calves and winced in disgust. Judging by her reaction, I think she convinced herself it was liquid turd. We sat down in a restaurant and Rueben promptly rested his forehead on the table and fell into a deep sleep and was only roused by a plate of hot chips. The other two children refused to eat anything local and devoured fried chicken and vegetables. Only Mary and I ate a local curry. On the road outside, motorbikes with side cars converted into stalls were parked up in rows on both sides of the street. Most sold fresh pancakes or fruit shakes, but a few sold edible beetles and one was converted into a pub complete with lights and music.

That night we fell into bed and slept almost immediately. As I drifted into sleep, I thought about the day. Compared to other first days in Asia, I was struck by how strangely joyless it was. I think we were all so tired that our internal wiring felt incapable of carrying enough power to create any sense of joy.

@@@@@

We were some of the first people to walk down the sandy road that led to Ta Phrom the next morning. It was still early and the jungle on both sides of the path hummed with life that sounded strangely like a car with squeaky brakes. Occasionally I heard the shrill call of a bird and once I looked above me and saw a large toucan silhouetted against the clear blue sky.

When Mary and I travelled through Thailand twenty years before, I remember first seeing Tha Phrom on a leaflet in Bangkok and I was enthralled by the images of an ancient temple eaten away by the jungle. Mary and I considered crossing into Cambodia at that point to see the temple but did not have enough money. It took two decades to step foot on that path, but finally I was about to see Tha Phrom. In those intervening years, the temple took on the street name of 'Tomb Raider temple' after Angelina Jolie immortalised it on the big screen by parachuting down into the area in her Land Rover and then chasing small children through the ruins.

"Dad I need some water," Evan asked. His bottom lip stuck out and he looked miserable.

I looked at Evan. Even though it was before eight o'clock in the morning, sweat dripped down his cheek and he looked like he had just run a few miles. I doubted I would be chasing any of my children around Tha Phrom.

"Sure Evan."

I grabbed a bottle from my backpack, handed it to him and then slowly walked on. Selfishly, after twenty years of waiting to see this temple, I was not going to let heat or thirsty children with water demands quench my anticipation.

I saw Tha Phrom for the first time. In truth I was a little disappointed at my first sighting; a yellow crane stood just high enough to extend a boom over the wall and out towards me. I hurried on, hoping that the inside would not disappoint.

It did not. The ruins were stunning. We wandered through passageways and into courtyards covered in jungle and fallen masonry. Ancient walls and towers were covered in lime-coloured moss. Almost every sandstone face was carved with decorative flower borders, many had carved facades of stunning women with serene faces and breasts the shape of pudding bowls. Ornate lingams broke through the jungle, most leant to the side due to age and the movement of the jungle trees. Buttress roots grew over the walls and buildings and provided some of the most beautiful and photographed vistas of Angor Wat historic park. Even though it was early, every time I lined up a shot, I always seemed to have an older lady or her husband wearing khaki pants photobombing my pictures.

At first the children seemed happy and so I wandered off to soak up the atmosphere before the tour buses and crowds arrived. I could have spent hours in that temple. Suddenly I realised that there was no sign of any family member, nor had there been for some time. I returned to the last place I saw Mary and the children. It took me some minutes to find them. To my surprise, Carrie, Evan and Rueben sat in a dark sheltered stone corridor and looked like they had been forced on a geography trip whilst suffering from a fever.

"Have you finished taking photos?" Mary asked.

"Yeah Dad. I'm hot," Rueben said.

Carrie looked up at me and scowled. "We've got a perfectly adequate pool at the hotel. Why are we here?"

"Come on everyone! Dad and Mum have paid a lot of money to get us all here. We are standing in one of the most loved buildings in the world. How can you not enjoy it?" I responded.

My mind went back to the moment half a year before when I announced I had purchased tickets to take us to Cambodia.

"Why can't we go to Spain like most normal people?" Carrie snapped back.

Looking at my children huddled in a stone tunnel, I wondered if she saw this as my punishment for making them come to another sweaty destination to look at old things.

"Come on Dave, it might be interesting for you, but

look at them all. All they want is the pool," Mary added.

I looked at them all. They all did look as bored as a person too small to go on any rides at a theme park.

"So, have you finished?" Mary asked.

Again, Mary used her ability of making a statement sound like a question.

As we left the temple and walked along the sand path back to our remork, Rueben crouched down and spent minutes looking at lines of insects that looked half ant and half scorpion. These ferocious-looking beasts worked together to carry far larger insects down into their snake hole shaped nest. Carrie and Evan joined him around the hole.

I felt a little sore with everyone. Having wanted to fully explore and enjoy this temple and waited twenty years, I was unimpressed having been bundled out of it. However, Carrie looked at the snake hole where the ants disappeared into and made me focus on a matter I had never considered before.

She asked, "Dad, do snakes poo?"

@@@@@

Suryavarman II was not first in line to be king. His parents were rulers of a provincial state in a Khmer Empire in decline. If this was the equivalent of the British Royal family, then this man had as much chance as getting onto the throne as Princess Beatrice. In short, the only way he could get to the top was to have a cull of those above him. A little over half a century after the William the Conqueror marched on London in 1066, Suryavarman II also went on a conquest.

His first kill was probably a key rival that went by the unpronounceable name of Nripatindravarman (who also had a good claim for the top job). Suryavarman II first killed the man with the long name, and then successfully murdered his great uncle and king, called Dharanindravarman. In one of these murders, he fought a battle where one inscription suggested he managed to get to his victim by leaping onto the elephant that his adversary was riding; a statement that is either an exaggeration or a description of a man who had supernatural strength, since such a leap from the ground has only ever been accomplished by men wearing rocket packs. Whatever the method, it is clear the man killed to get to the throne and achieve his goal. Suryavararman II was clearly a driven man.

A driven man who kills to get power usually has a big ego and Suryavarman II was a man who believed in leaving his mark on the world. When he realised that his time on the planet was limited, he corralled thousands (perhaps tens of thousands) of his subjects for half a decade to clear the forest, dig trenches and erect the largest religious building in the world – Angkor Wat.

@@@@@

Unlike Tha Phrom and other temples in the area that sat in jungle foliage, Angor Wat had almost no shade. Having seen a few temples that morning, we were tired, and the temperature left us wilting and in bad humour. The walk from the car park across a pontoon that crossed the moat to the temple itself was particularly punishing. There were hordes of tourists. Angkor Wat is one of the jewels in the crown in the whistle stop tours of south-east Asia and I was worried that we would lose small children if we got separated. Carrie stormed ahead as her mother, her brothers and I struggled along a raised stone path that led to the temples.

"Carrie can you walk with us please?" I asked.

She ignored me.

"Carrie! Don't walk ahead. I don't want to lose you

in the crowds."

She dropped back a little but then carried on walking quickly ahead.

"Right that's it. You have lost twenty minutes in the pool!"

"Fine!" She retorted and turned around to continue her march to some shade.

Now that the punishment was clear, there was nothing I could do to slow her down.

In the heat, we looked like a family that did not like each other. I turned to look at the boys and even though they were silent, I knew they thought that I was acting unfairly. They looked at me like they were victims of a big bully. I knew that they too considered walking around a temple, with almost no shade in an infernal dampness, was an act of pointless endeavour when there was a perfectly adequate pool to swim in.

"And why on earth are there so many people obsessed with posing!" I spat the words out as I stepped around a group who abruptly stopped in front of us.

There were thousands of Asian tourists stopping in doorways; posing for a photo on their smartphones, smiling and pouting whilst looking over their shoulders like pretend fashion models. Out of spite, I did my best to get in their photos and turn around to ensure my displeasure was recorded.

It suddenly occurred to me that it was mostly me who seemed affected by the heat.

With this realisation, I suggested that we find some shade, something everyone agreed with. We found a quiet corner to sit away from crowds and had the company of a row of Buddha statues that mostly had no heads, but a few also had no feet. It was an opportunity for me to calm down and apologise to Carrie.

"Dad I need a wee!" Rueben suddenly announced with a look of alarmed urgency.

I looked at the map and realised the toilet was in a similar direction to that from which we had just come. Evan, Rueben and I stormed along a stone corridor full of carvings of elephants, monkeys and men with what looked like dragons flying out of their pants and left the temple complex at one corner. A guard pointed us to what looked like a bank of trees but was really a bustling village, hidden from view.

We followed painted signs to a toilet and came across an outbuilding on the edge of the village. The toilet was a traditional squat affair with an adjacent bin full of used sanitary towels and toilet paper. The flush was a cup in a water tank. After he was relieved, Rueben leant against the wall next to the bin, oblivious to what he stood next to. I dragged him away.

Rueben standing at a pool that reflects Angkor Wat

"Oh, Evan please hurry up!"
My eyes watered as acidic clouds of hot urine stung

my eyes.

"Just wait outside and let me finish," Evan retorted.

This was something I gladly did. I thought about Carrie wincing with some splattered mud against her leg the previous night.

"This toilet would have been the stuff of nightmares for you," I muttered to myself, thankful she was not with me.

That afternoon I sat by the hotel pool. Carrie never did have twenty minutes less in the water since I realised that my ranting was more about me overheating than her doing anything wrong. The children created jumps based on the life of Moses. However, this came to an end when Rueben belly-flopped and declared it was Moses and the burning bush and created such water displacement that Evan was briefly blinded.

Carrie played happily with the boys and then went back to the room without any warning. She probably remembered that such games were too juvenile for her to enjoy. I thought about her behaviour in the temples (and mine) and realised that over the last few months she often forgot where she put things or just put them in the wrong place. Earlier that day, I asked her to bring her phone inside the hotel room but even after several prompts it sat cooking in the Asian heat on the balcony outside and looked easy to steal. She left a glass of half-drunk water on the tiled floor; a perfect place for someone to kick and tear open their feet on the broken glass. She could not remember where she left her swimming costume. It took her five minutes to locate it; bunched up and left half-hidden behind her parent's bed. I thought about her anxious declaration that she had a mosquito bite the previous night. She told us in the same way she would declare the loss of a little finger or even worse, her phone. Carrie was a teenager; sometimes a little adult with child tendencies, and sometimes a little child with adult tendencies.

I thought about the way I snapped on the path to Angor Wat. All she wanted was some shade and as an adult she made a choice to walk faster to get some comfort. I saw her as a child and was worried about her getting lost. As I sat by the pool, I realised that it was not her who needed to change. Being a teenager is a rite of passage. As her Dad it was time for me to adjust.

Carrie and Rueben at the pool in Siem Reap

@@@@@

That evening we took a remork and were dropped off at a wooden footbridge that crossed the Tonle Sap river. A group of men played a game that looked a little like 'hacky sack'. This game, however, was played with a plastic stick that looked a little like a German grenade from World War Two. The players watched the toy as it floated past their head and then timed a kick from behind their back to send it flying back into the air to their opponent.

"Dad they could be footballers being able to do that!" Rueben shouted after a few moments of rapture at the player's dexterity.

We were starving, and along the river were street vendors with motorcycle sidecars converted into portable kitchens that sold noodles and soups. It took a few minutes wandering along the row of bikes to find an eating place that we all liked. Then we sat down on children's chairs and waited for bowls of pork, rice and big noodle soup to be served to us. We sat next to an overflowing bin and normally such circumstances would be unpleasant, but it was lovely because it was a perfect place to people watch. Carrie and I ordered the same thing. My soup had lumps of potato and carrot and brown cubic things of what (I think) was liver.

"Dad what is this?" Carrie asked as she held up a brown cube with her chopsticks.

"I think it's a local version of tofu," I told her in the hope she would eat it.

"You are such a liar," she laughed and placed the brown things into my bowl.

After dinner, we purchased pancakes and sat on a wooden bridge that was lit up by fluorescent lights and enjoyed the cool evening breeze. In the distance lightning flashed, but it never rained like the previous day. We returned to the hotel and swam in the pool in the darkness and fell asleep after watching a surreal National Geographic program about a man who discovered ship wrecks based on information given to him by an astronaut.

There were two rival empires that had regular fights in south-east Asia around nine hundred years ago; the Chams and Khmers. The paint on Angkor Wat was barely dry in 1150AD, when the Chams took a boat trip from their strongholds in modern day Vietnam, sailed up the Mekong, into the giant Tonle Sap lake and up the Tonle Sap river to Angkor Wat. They killed the ruling Khmer king and ransacked the city. As a defeated and occupied nation, the Khmers needed a hero and Jayavarman VII delivered that in bucket loads. Just one year after the invasion, he led a Khmer army and kicked out the Chams, and it was this victory that put him on the path to becoming king.

Whilst outsiders considered his victory over the Chams as the highlight of his life, King Jayavarman may have considered marrying two sisters as his greatest conquest. The sisters were Buddhists and it was them that probably inspired Jayavarman to become a Buddhist himself. Jayavarman was a good king. In his thirty-year reign, he focussed on building roads, rest houses, hospitals and built one of the loveliest temples in the Angkor Wat temple area. It is situated in the middle of his city called Angkor Thom and is called Bayon.

Jayavarman liked Bayon. He liked it so much that he placed his image all over the towers; smiling out at his subjects. Five hundred years later, Bayon provides some of the most iconic images of the Angkor Wat historical site.

@@@@@

In the early morning light, the chaotic columns, well-manicured fallen masonry and the towers with their faces looked stunning. As we walked through the temple gates, Rueben, Evan and Carrie were thrilled to see baby monkeys suckling on mothers and sitting on the uneven grey steps. Carrie took photos with her phone, and Evan and Rueben fought over my phone to record the animals. Unlike at Angkor Wat, it was early and despite it being one of the most popular temples to see, few people were around.

We walked through dark corridors and over uneven steps. Even in the gloom, I saw the walls were covered in decorative carvings from floor to ceiling and in a few places, the paint they used to add life to the carvings could still be seen. Finally, we climbed to the top of the tower to look onto the famous smiling stone faces that made this temple so famous. Surrounded by green jungle, the lingam-shaped towers with their smiling faces looked stunning even after a thousand years. Carrie thought that some of them looked like creepy clowns.

One of the famous faces of Jayavarman on Bayon temple

The children happily walked about photographing monkeys. I looked at the photos the boys took later that day. Most of the photos on my phone were grainy or blurred. The clearest one was taken by Evan – a picture of a monkey's bottom. It was a relief to visit a temple that the children seemed to enjoy, and their enjoyment left me free to wander and look at the famous smiling rock carvings. Some of the faces appeared to have a genuine smile and others seemed to be a little forced; as if someone had recently broken wind in their company but they needed to keep up appearances.

Bayon was a surprise to me. Many people seemed to mention Angkor Wat and Bayon in the same breath and I wrongly assumed they were similar. Angkor Wat looks symmetrically perfect and scrubbed clean whereas Bayon from a distance looked like a ruined building covered in wax. I know which one I preferred.

We walked on to the neighbouring temple called Baphuon. It was taken apart by a team of well-meaning archaeologists in the 1970s to add support to the base. However, shortly after dismantling was complete and all the blocks carefully laid out and numbered, the Khmer Rouge came along and lost the plans. However, Baphuon is back together now.

Mary, Rueben and Carrie struggled in the heat and so only Evan and I went to climb Baphoun. We walked along the raised brick path and realised that our tickets to allow us to climb were with Mary. Evan ran back (two hundred metres in the heat) grabbed the bags and came back to me, only for the guard to tell me that Evan was "too small to climb" as the steps were so steep.

The whole experience was not wasted though. I gained a deep satisfaction watching a French family with two young boys wilting in the heat and debating whether they should give up on the temples. The man gesticulated towards the stairs and his wife and sons looked on as if he had just announced Christmas was cancelled. I took comfort in the fact that other families also struggled in the tedium of temples.

It did not take long to get away from crowds at Angkor Thom. We wandered along dusty grass to ruined buildings and saw butterflies with wings so large they glided rather than fluttered. The only sound I heard was Rueben dragging a stick, the sound of crickets in the jungle and the brush of foliage as a sunning lizard dove for cover as we approached.

The Gates of Angkor Thom

We exited the gate of Angkor Thom with its smiling benevolent face on stone arches that spanned the road, and headed to Preah Khan. Preah Khan is a temple with corridors that seemed to go on for kilometres. At regular intervals there were courtyards full of rubble; tablets of intricate carvings of dancing ladies and ornate friezes lay around in glorious decay. In the middle of one corridor was an altar with an enormous smoothed tablet-shaped stone in the middle of an altar with channels carved into the top.

"Dad what's this for?" Rueben asked

"It is a stone willy. Quite often water would be poured over the lingam and then collected by women to help with fertility."

I felt quite knowledgeable as I said it but only knew this fact because I heard a guide say it. Carrie looked at me, laughed and blushed.

Rueben ran up to Mary shouting, "Mum! Mum! There is a stone willy here!" It was as if he had just discovered a mountain of chocolate under a rock.

That evening, we sat by the bins on the roadside again and ate dinner. Afterwards, we sat on the bridge, enjoyed the cool breeze, ate pancakes and drank fruit shakes. Evan sat with his legs crossed and looked in some discomfort because he needed a poo. He claimed his impending bowel movement was brought on by his cold mango fruit shake.

Whilst the breeze over the river refreshed, our ears were assaulted by two competing bands playing a few metres from each other. On one side of the bridge was a group that played traditional Cambodian music; most of the people appeared to be missing limbs. On the other side of the bridge was a local Hare Krishna band. When they both played together, it sounded like fairground music having an accident. The louder one group went, the louder the other group was forced to go.

That evening Rueben spent an hour before bed practicing Bollywood dancing. Carrie gave him some direction that the movement of his hands should be like he was changing a lightbulb. We all fell asleep watching 'Naked and Afraid', one of the greatest television programs that I consider has ever been produced. The premise is that two strangers (a male and female) remove their clothes, are then dumped together in a jungle environment and forced to survive.

@@@@@

In 1953, Cambodia gained full independence from France, and at first all seemed well in this area of the world. Prince Norodom Sihanouk was elected head of the country with a vibrant culture that encouraged modern music and parties. The fun, however, was not to last. A coup that saw Sihanouk removed from power, and the Vietnam War that kept creeping over the Cambodian border created a perfect condition for a Marxist guerrilla group to seize control of the country. The Khmer Rouge rolled into Phnom Penh in April 1975 and were greeted by many as heroes.

The celebration lasted just a few hours and over the next five years, the country was renamed, the cities were cleared of all people and around a quarter of the population were killed. Then in 1979, Cambodia was invaded by Vietnam after a series of border clashes. The Khmer Rouge was forced back to the border near Thailand and the Vietnamese did not leave for the next fourteen years.

The Khmer Rouge planted landmines partly to control the population from escaping and partly to protect the country from the Vietnamese. After the Vietnamese entered, they too contributed to the landmine tally. No one kept a map of where the mines were planted, and the consequence today is that the country has one of the highest amputee rates in the world caused by landmines.

In 2013, one hundred and eleven people were killed or injured by mines that have sat around in the Cambodian countryside for thirty years. To break down that statistic, in the three weeks we spent in Cambodia, seven people would be maimed or killed by landmines, many of them boys. With an estimated four to six million landmines still left in Cambodia, this is a tragedy that is unlikely to go away anytime soon.

Aki Ra was not certain when he was born; sometime in 1970 or 1973. He never knew his parents because they were killed by the Khmer Rouge. They then brought Aki Ra up to be a child soldier; teaching him how to fire a gun and the art of jungle warfare. However, his time with the Khmer Rouge did not last and when the Vietnamese army turned up, he defected and fought against his former Khmer Rouge units. At night, the Vietnamese sent him out to hunt for animals in the jungle and there he met up with his former Khmer Rouge friends. They hunted together and once they had enough, they played together. The following day, they tried to kill each other, such was the surreal nature of the war.

After his fighting career was over, he found employment as a de-miner with the United Nations but left after one year. However, he continued disarming and removing land mines using a knife, a hoe, a stick and a Swiss army knife. Tourists heard about Aki Ra and he realised the potential of charging a few dollars to see his latest collection of empty mine casings to fund support for landmine survivors. It was this collection that turned into the Cambodian Landmine Museum.

When we visited, the entrance looked tired, with a short avenue of rusting warheads in the place where most people would expect to see bollards. Once inside, the place continued to look a little ramshackle with dummies dressed as solders that looked like they could be candidates for scarecrows. However, the stories and messages were clear, uplifting and tragic in equal measures. Above all, it was a great introduction to the recent history of Cambodia.

I walked around the hut that contained panels that told stories about the young landmine victims and struggled to hold back tears. There was a story about one child who thought the mine was a toy and took it apart.

As he attempted to reassemble the weapon, it detonated and blew off his arm. Another board told the story of a child whose friends picked up a mine in the belief that it looked like a toy pineapple. When it exploded, their friends were killed instantly and the victim telling the story lost a leg (even though he stood twenty metres away from the blast).

Whilst I read these accounts, my children sat and grimaced as the sun and the heat got the better of them. I do not think they felt any sense of sadness at the testimonies like I did. I looked at them as they sat with their heads in their hands, and initially felt irritated by their disinterest.

"You don't realise how unbelievably fortunate you are," I thought.

I remembered they wilted in the heat the previous day; it was hotter and stickier than a road worker's armpit at the end of a summer's day, and it was not unreasonable to be struggling in those temperatures.

I returned to reading the boards but a few moments later, I looked over again at my children once more. They sat quietly in the shade and squinted as they looked out into the harsh daylight; waiting without any complaint for Mary and I to finish reading.

I took a deep breath. It dawned on me that getting irritated with them was certainly not the way. That happened a few days before at Angkor Wat and the results were ugly.

"Besides," I thought, "would a landmine museum have interested me as a teenager?"

I promised myself that as soon as we were back in Siem Reap, I would treat them to a refreshing coke or a smoothie and talk with them about what I read.

Chapter 2: Battambang

The next day we arrived in Battambang. Grown men desperately banged on the windows of the bus and held up laminate cards advertising free rides to hotels. As a family, the earning potential they saw in us meant we were given the most fervent attention.

"You get the kids off and I'll get the bag," I said to Mary.

I hated being met by taxi drivers as I stepped off buses with the children and luggage. I usually found my heart raced as I dragged the bags off the bus, made sure the children were safe and dealt with hopeful enquiries about our names or where we intend to stay simultaneously. It always felt like my duty to negotiate prices and select the driver. My coping strategy was to smile and laugh even though I wanted to tell the drivers to get lost.

This time, though, I was surprised and relieved that by the time I placed the main backpack over my shoulder and turned around, Mary was chatting to an older gentleman standing a little distance from the crowd. The children were already sitting in a remork.

"He works for the hotel we've booked," Mary said smiling.

"Hello, I'm David," I said and held out my hand for him to shake it.

"Sann." He shook my hand and bowed; laughing a little at the novelty of a Western greeting that to me felt as instinctive as bowing was to Sann. Looking back, I think he was a little taken back by my enthusiasm. He did not recognise that I felt relieved that I had got away from the taxi driver negotiations so easily. If there had not been a handshake then I probably would have given the air a little punch, and that would have looked weird and perhaps a little frightening to this tranquil man.

Sann dropped us at the hotel and we arranged for him to take us to the Bamboo Train later in the afternoon. We unpacked at the hotel and swam in the pool, drying off in the heat even though thunder rumbled in the distance and thick grey clouds threatened a heavy monsoon shower.

The Bamboo Train is a section of the old French-built railway that ran from the Thai border, across to Phnom Penh and ended at the coast at Sihanoukville. At the time of the Khmer Rouge, much of the line fell into disrepair and no trains ran on it for many years. However, during the Vietnamese occupation, and with little money and a good deal of endeavour, the local people created makeshift carriages that they pushed along the rails to transport goods. Later in the 1980s the locals attached petrol motors and a makeshift drive belt and then the carriages could travel at up to fifty miles per hour. In Battambang, a few enterprising people decided to charge tourists to travel on these carriages, and soon the Bamboo Train was a fixture on the tourist route.

According to the World Bank, Cambodia's economy since the millennium has had a growth rate in the top ten percent of all nations. Rail is now seen by the Cambodian government as key infrastructure for continuing the economic growth. Whilst there are routine delays in such projects, many predict that the death knell for this tourist experience will soon be heard as the line is modernised.

As we travelled to the outskirts of town, thunder rumbled ahead of us and the sky turned a menacing grey. I looked up at the clouds and wondered if this trip would be better taken the following day as I knew that the train was exposed to the elements. However, the children looked forward to the novelty of getting propelled along a track at thirty miles per hour whilst sitting on a bamboo mat and so was I, so I kept quiet.

At the station closest to Battambang, Sann led us to the railway and spoke a few words to a man who appeared to be in charge.

"One family, twenty dollars," the man said.

I was glad that I did not have to deal with the drivers, since they all looked like modern-day pirates. The driver that the controller assigned us had a silver tooth. I only noticed it when he grimaced the first time he needed to exert energy, rather than when he smiled (which he never did).

The children sat at the front and Mary and I sat on the back of a bamboo platform that was the size of a double bed. Travelling at speed on a bamboo platform with nothing to hold on to was a little unnerving, particularly when the train tracks seemed a little misaligned through age and the carriage jolted with little warning. We flew along with views over bush and paddy fields and I was regularly whipped by foliage.

After a mile or so, we approached the end station. Judging by the large volume of ladies looking down the line towards us carrying t-shirts and trinkets, I knew that we were about to endure some hard selling.

I turned and told the children, "Right this looks like a big tourist trap. They are going to go in hard to sell us stuff, so do not look interested."

"Get off and stay for ten minutes," the driver said, "you sit there."

He pointed at a shaded picnic table. It was the only time he spoke with us. As the train stopped, we jumped off; compliant under his grumpy demeanour. A lady smiled at us and led us to the shaded picnic table. Her smile seemed more sinister than friendly. Immediately she placed a bowl of threaded bracelets in front of the children.

"You want bracelet?" the lady asked with a nasally voice.

"Yeah!" Rueben responded with such enthusiasm that the woman laughed as if she had hit a seam of gold.

Evan on the Battambang train

My instruction to not show interest seemed to be forgotten by Rueben. Soon t-shirts and toy bamboo trains appeared, brought to us by a steady stream of gnarled women. Above the table, I had to navigate my way through an army of sellers. Below the table, a scrawny chicken and a cockerel had a minor domestic argument and continually pecked at my sandals.

The train runs on a single track and so each time carriages approach from different directions, the carriage with the least amount of people cedes to the one with the most. On the return journey, however, this rule was not followed. Each time we met a carriage, it was always us that was made to disembark so that the two meeting drivers could haul our bamboo platform onto the side of the railroad and remove the heavy axel and wheels so that the train travelling in the opposite direction could pass.

Mary became irritated about this rigmarole, as if it was done to us on purpose. I was happy to stop, because in the distance, the last rays of sun shone through the black clouds and onto flat paddy fields, turning them lime green. I considered the view spectacular and if I was travelling at thirty miles an hour on a bamboo platform then I would have missed the vista and a great photographic opportunity.

At the end of the ride, a worker asked, "You enjoy the ride – yes?"

"Yes, very much," I responded.

It would be churlish for me to have said no, but I knew what was going to come.

"Then you pay this man a tip."

I wanted to tell the man to go away since I paid twenty dollars to enjoy the ride and purchased bracelets at the stop. I gave our driver a dollar and am sure he said something derogatory to me that made a nearby local laugh. I suspect it was on the lines of a fruit-flavoured curse in Khmer.

Did I enjoy the bamboo train? Yes. Did I make any local friends on the way? Absolutely not.

@@@@@

The following day Sann took us on his 'handicraft tour'. We drove along pot-holed roads lined with banana trees, jungle foliage and traditional houses built on stilts. The houses had blue shutters closed over the windows to keep out the sun. Children played and chatted together on the roadside and when we passed them, they waved and greeted us as if we were famous.

"In Battambang no English children!" Sann shouted over the motorbike engine to us, glancing over the top of his sunglasses that made him look a little like 'Knight Rider'.

Our first stop with Sann was at a wooden shack with an open front on the side of the road. Three women sat resting, and a newborn baby wearing a woolly hat slept in a hammock. On the back wall, lines of bamboo stumps sat on a shelf just above some smouldering charcoal. For the whole previous day, we wondered what these bamboo stumps were. The minibus driver that took us from Siem Reap to Battambang confused us when he stopped and purchased what we thought was a just a piece of bamboo. Since then, we regularly saw women sitting in temporary shelters on the roadside selling these stumps and we had no clue as to what they contained.

Sann explained that the tubes contain a delicious rice dish called 'Kralan'. It is made by placing sticky rice, black beans and carnation milk in the bamboo tube, and then the tube is baked in charcoal. The result was sold to road travellers as a healthy and cheap lunchbox. We purchased two tubes for two thousand riel (around fifty pence) and ate them after the tour; stripping away the bamboo and devouring the rice in five minutes. Disappointingly, we never saw this snack again. We were disappointed because they were cheap, healthy and above all the only vegetarian food that all the children loved, except margarita pizza and ice cream.

Sann then took us to a crocodile farm down an ochre-coloured dirt road. We walked up a driveway, past sleeping dogs, and weregreeted by a smiling lady who stood next to a tub of baby crocodiles. They made strange squeaking noises that made them sound like a 1980s computer game. Carrie, Mary and I cradled a crocodile as if it were a child though Rueben refused to hold one. Evan was pressed into holding a reptile by Sann and the smiling host, but immediately dropped it in fear. It was thankfully caught by Sann just before its beady little eye and snout hit the pavement.

Next, Sann took us over to the big cages that contained the fully-grown crocodiles. They sat frozen and immobile and to get them to move, Sann prodded them in the stomach with a large stick. The action had its desired effect and they retaliated with an irritated hiss, a baring of teeth and swish of the tail. We walked above them, along the concrete walls that separated the tanks. A thin metal rail the width of a Cumberland sausage was the only barrier that stopped us from falling in and getting torn apart.

"Mary make sure you hold onto Evan's hand!" I barked in fear as I grabbed Rueben's.

I was concerned my middle son was going to stumble with his endearing clumsiness and disappear over the gangplank.

"It's amazing that such a small baby can grow into something so big," Evan said gently. Clearly, he was not as concerned about his propensity to stumble as I.

"Evan stop looking around you and keep looking at where you put your feet!" I shouted at him.

In a pond on the other side of the wall we saw the eyes of an escaped crocodile eyeing up some locals standing at the side. Sann shouted over a warning but the locals waved back as if they knew about the threat and carried on working. Safety was not too high on the agenda at the farm.

After the farm visit, we stopped at a ruined Khmer temple just outside the town that sat behind an enormous Buddha. The ruins were covered in blood-red scrub. It was so hot that it was difficult to truly appreciate the place, but the cats in the vicinity with their kinked tails kept Carrie and Rueben amused and dismayed in equal measure. A litter of kittens came over to say hello, though one of them was so weak she barely lifted her head, crawled into the shade of the remork and refused to move. Both Carrie and Rueben tried to feed it some rice, but it did not seem interested. By the time Mary, Evan and I returned, Carrie and Rueben were all set to take it home and see it restored to health.

"Please Dad, can we?" they both pleaded.

Mary and I agreed there was almost no chance of us changing the outcome even if we could find a vet.

To finish the tour, Sann took us to a temple compound that was named Wat Samrong Knong. At first, I was struck by the new golden Buddha reaching high into the boiling cobalt blue sky. It stood at odds to the other buildings and statues in the area that looked in need of a paint or were chipped and covered in mould. We parked up under a tree next to what our guide said was a temple, now locked up. It was a wooden building covered in peeling paint and had thick cobwebs in the cracks. Sann said it used to be a temple but was converted into a prison by the Khmer Rouge to house prisoners after they cleared Battambang of its entire population.

It was hard imagining what it was like just forty years before; full of frightened people. All I heard as I stood looking at the double doors locked shut was the hum of insects in the grass. I wondered what tales the cobwebs in the cracks could tell but did not have the time to dwell on such matters as Sann led us away towards a pond. The pond looked more like a small crater in the ground filled with reeds, but he thought it important to point it out.

Next door to the pond was an ornate memorial in the shape of a tower. About halfway up I saw human skulls and bones laid out in a cage. This was the first macabre evidence I saw with my own eyes of the genocide committed by the Khmer Rouge.

"Are you OK for young ones to see this?" Sann

asked as he pointed to Evan, Rueben and the cage.

It was a question that Mary and I asked many times before coming to Cambodia. Do we hide the atrocities of the Khmer Rouge from the children? Or do we allow them to hear and see things and then gauge their reaction? We decided to do the latter and allow them to be exposed to the difficult chapter of Cambodian history and act only if they were upset or frightened.

The monument that contained the bones was engraved in English and Khmer and told us about the clearance of Battambang by the Khmer Rouge and about children who were thrown into the air and cruelly pinned by soldiers holding spears as they fell to the ground. Just over ten thousand people were slaughtered in this location; many were killed by suffocation using plastic bags over their heads and then dumped in the pond we had just passed. Some of the prisoners were bound together by putting holes in the hands and using the wounds as tethering points. A few were decapitated by using the sharp end of a palm leaf.

Sann talked, elaborating on the information panels of the monument and telling us about the Khmer's extensive use of child soldiers. My mind raced; perhaps this was a bit much for the children and I wanted to politely change the scene.

Evan then asked Sann a question that most adults would be too polite to ask.

"How old are you?"

"Evan! You cannot ask people that question!" I chided him gently.

Sann ignored me. He told Evan he had just turned fifty. I saw Evan look up just like he did when he was doing his maths homework.

"So, if you were a child at the time, were you fighting for the Khmer Rouge?" Evan asked.

Sann looked at Evan. For a moment he was

surprised at the question. Mary and I were not certain if we should scold him or feel proud of him.

Sann smiled at Evan. "Very, very lucky."

Sann told us about his experiences, how he stole every night as he was starving, of being separated from his brothers, sisters and parents. Unlike so many families, none of his immediate family were killed. Even though they were separated, they all found each other after the war. Twice he was caught stealing; once for climbing a tree and taking a coconut. The other time he stole a pumpkin and was spotted but managed to escape his masters through luck and being a faster runner than the soldier.

"Very lucky," he repeated, still smiling

Carrie looked at me, took a deep breath, "All these old people we see, they probably have their own story about this time."

I looked at Carrie and smiled. It was great to see her engaged.

"So, Mum, if I get a palm leaf, did you know, I could cut your head off?" Rueben said, clearly more interested in the mechanics of the cruelty rather than its effects.

That evening we drove out to Phnom Sampeau, a local landmark and hill about half an hour from Battambang along a straight and very flat road. The hill had a sprinkling of interesting things; nice views, temples, some history, caves and a natural spectacle at twilight. As we drove, there was a bit of thunder, but the cloud and breeze cooled us.

Like all inclines in south-east Asia, Rueben refused to walk and insisted I carried him. About halfway up we came to a Buddhist temple. Rueben had not quite got the grasp of Buddhism and asked me, "Dad, what is this Buddha called?"

I took photos of the prayer flags whilst Evan asked

Sann why the Cambodian people thought the Khmer Rouge were so good at the beginning. I wanted to hear his answer, but Rueben would not stand still and so I missed what Sann said.

Just beyond the temple, we wandered past a graphic betrayal of hell in the form of a series of sculptures. Sann explained that the sculptures were meant to remind people of what the Khmer Rouge would face in the afterlife. According to the sculptures, adulterous people would be forced to climb on top of a cactus wearing no clothes and, when fully ascended, endure the pain of a man shoving a spear into the anus. Those who drank would have a wine bottle shoved so far into their mouth their mouths split open and blood would pour out. Those that lied would have their tongue taken out with pliers. Rueben was intrigued by a woman whose head was getting sliced open by a chainsaw, but Sann had no idea what crime warranted this punishment.

The mountain we climbed is arguably most famous for the killing cave. In the 1970s, an estimated two thousand people were bludgeoned to death and thrown into a cave via a skylight by the Khmer Rouge. The single saving grace was that many of the people were killed before they were dropped. We approached the cave by walking down stairs bordered by waxy and luscious green jungle vegetation. As it was late in the afternoon, the high pitch sound of mosquitoes left us swatting at our necks.

When the Vietnamese pushed back the Khmer Rouge, the locals took the remains of the victims and stored them in a cage in the cave that looked a little like a chicken coop. Foreign money allowed a more dignified shelter and a statue of a reclining Buddha to be created, and now many of the remains sat inside a decorative glass cage.

As we descended into the cave, Rueben looked at the reclining Buddha.

"Dad is that a dead body?" he whispered loudly.

A local teenage girl heard him and burst into laughter at Rueben's innocent question.

After we left the cave, we stood and looked over the flat green plains with Sann. He told me he fought with the Vietnamese army in the 1990s when the fighting with the Khmer Rouge was in its decline, but that did not diminish the horrors he saw. A friend of his was seriously wounded by a landmine and he carried him for several days on a stretcher, but his friend died just before he reached help. Once back in civilisation, rather than returning to the fight, Sann asked for a few days off to see his family and rest. However, when he got home, he decided to never return to the battle. He paid a smuggler to get him across the Thai border where he lived in a UNHCR refuge until the fighting stopped.

"I saw the Khmer Rouge execute people on two occasions," he said after a pause and pointed at a football field at the foot of the mountain. "I was invited to a football game on false pretences and was forced to watch the murder of eight people."

We all stood silently for a few moments after Sann spoke. Even Evan did not have the heart to ask why or how.

Nearby, two monks sat and chatted by a golden painted Buddha sitting amongst some trees. As I passed by one of them they started chanting 'om mani padme hum' in a voice that sounded just like Elvis Priestly. Rueben and Sann spent five minutes trying to copy the hand positions of the Buddha statue. Rueben managed it in the end, but not before many attempts that made his hand look slightly arthritic, much to Sann's amusement.

We climbed up to the pagodas at the top of the mountain and looked again over the views that in the setting sun were postcard perfect. All around us, paddy fields stretched out across to the horizon with single forested hills the only part of the landscape that did not appear straight or flat. We could see over twenty kilometres when we stood on a platform that was meant to be a lookout.

I think the lookout was only half made because exposed metal poles stuck out of the reinforced concrete floor and there was no barrier despite the sheer drop. Rueben and Evan were more interested leaning out over the edge and looking at the litter-coated jungle and the ash piles below rather than the view. I enjoyed the view, but irrational visions of the boys falling from the lookout and getting speared by the tree tops or getting an open head wound that was made worse by pawing monkeys meant I never truly relaxed.

Mary on the summit of Phnom Sampeau

Carrie refused to look around the top of the hill, so she sat and waited for us. Whilst she waited, a mosquito bit her in the small of her nose. As we walked down the hill, she insisted on wearing a hat even though the sting of the sun was well passed. I suspected she was embarrassed by the bite and teased her gently; suggesting that a single bump may be mistaken for a little horn.

"Some people may think you are a unicorn" I added after a few moments.

She ignored my comment.

We climbed down the steps to the main road and sat opposite a large gash in the cliff. By the time we arrived just before sunset, hundreds of people sipped beers and sat at cheap red picnic tables waiting for the best show in town to begin. As we were a little late, there was nowhere to sit and so we perched on a wall and ate raw bread. The children fed most of the last slice to two skeletal cats. I think they were motivated mostly out of boredom rather than generosity.

The sun fell below the horizon and the show was about to begin, but much to the children's irritation, nature followed no human clock.

"Dad I'm hungry," Evan whinged as he watched the two cats eat the last of the bread.

"Yeah Dad, when's dinner?" Rueben asked.

"Look there's one there!" I said as I pointed to the cave, trying to create a fake sense of excitement at the view of a cliff at sunset.

Finally, a single bat flew out. Suddenly, hundreds of black dots fired out of the crack and that quickly expanded to tens of thousands. It was a scene that reminded me of the winged monkeys in the 'Wizard of Oz'. To see this multitude of bats snaking their way across the sky and the fields left me open-mouthed. Just like in Sri Lanka with the elephants, I felt a strong urge to embrace anyone standing close to me. Even the boys forgot about their need to graze for a few moments as I high-fived the children and Mary in my nature-induced euphoria, though

I recall Carrie scowled a little as she reluctantly raised her hand in response.

"I'm not a unicorn," Carrie said.

Not for the first time on this trip I apologised to my daughter.

Back at the night market in the centre of town we ate dinner. I paid Sann thirty-three dollars. He asked for twenty-two for the day, but his stories and his company added so much to our experience. He smiled and bowed with his hands together in thanks as I gave him the money. I felt embarrassed to give it. He was a man far greater than I.

@@@@@

On our final day in Battambang we had a slower day. Rueben, Carrie, Evan and a three-year-old girl (whose parents ran the hotel) built flower shapes on the poolside using stones, leaves and flower petals. Each time the little girl handed a petal over to Carrie, the little girl said "*Hello?*". The little girl even handed me two peach-coloured petals. This was a rare event since small children are usually a little frightened of my loud voice and curly hair. I was at a loss as to what I should do with them and so held the leaves up to my ears and pretended to be a rabbit. The little girl stood back, a little amused but mostly frightened. It suddenly occurred to me that they may not have rabbits in Cambodia and therefore my impression must have looked truly odd.

At about three o'clock that afternoon, I was bored and looked for something to do. I decided we would all take a remork to the old train station. Mary went along with me as she was not willing to get involved with the children's antipathy towards such an excursion. Carrie, Evan and Rueben could not understand the purpose of leaving the cool of our room and the pool to endure such madness. They sat in the remork close to tears as enormous beads of sweat formed on their brows and temples.

"Come on guys there are loads of old trains we can see here."

Carrie glared at me.

"It will be fun!" I mumbled in hope.

The old train station had a modernist 1950s shape with a clock frozen at three minutes past eight. Our guidebook suggested making a visit to the station because the building was very pretty and there were beautiful but rusting French colonial trains parked in the adjacent sheds. However, when we arrived, the station forecourt was used as a place to park trucks and the only thing we saw in the empty railway sheds was an old man asleep in a hammock.

With the visit to the train station regarded as a failure, we walked to the town centre. On both sides of the street, old colonial buildings were converted into welding shops and garages and I had to look carefully to see any beauty. I doubt my family cared about the street scene as we trudged through thirty-five-degree heat. I walked ahead but I knew my children bristled with anger. They scowled at Mary and I, and the local children who greeted them were studiously ignored by all three. The only thing that acted as balm on their irritation was an iced coffee by the market.

If the day excursion was a failure, the evening was a huge turn for the better. I experienced one of the most uplifting events I have had in a long time; at the circus.

We sat on the front row on wooden benches made shiny by years of bottom-polishing. I had no expectations; the last time I went to the circus was on a rundown council estate just outside Liverpool. It was the 1980s and I recall they still had dancing bears.

The lights dimmed, and the music started. It was

provided by a shirtless but toned drummer wearing a brimless hat like those worn by Nepali men, and a xylophone player. From the opening note until the lights dimmed at the end, they gave their all to the music and by the end of the performance sweat covered the duo. The soundtrack to the whole performance reminded me of a 1930s Disney cartoon.

The acrobats used simple props like brooms with googly eyes attached to the bristles, and buckets. Using their simple props, childlike movements and acrobatic skill, they told us a tale about the small and insignificant people taking on a dictator. At the beginning, the people danced for joy for the dictator but in the end, he turned and destroyed them all. The sole woman of the troupe was the last to be destroyed and fought the hardest.

I sat next to Rueben in the performance and occasionally glanced at him. He sat open-mouthed and still throughout the show. His posture summed up how we all felt. At the end, his enthusiastic clapping reminded me of a North Korean on parade days, though Rueben was genuine. The skill in their dance and acrobatics mixed with humour, gentleness, joy and poignancy left us walking away with our arms around each other, laughing. Days later, Carrie and I admitted that we both still thought about that performance much of the time.

Chapter 3: Phnom Penh

The following day we purchased a five-dollar ticket to take us the two hundred kilometres from Battambang to Phnom Penh. Purple curtains hung at the front of the bus and a television was bolted to the roof in the centre above the aisle. A picture of the current king was stuck to the windscreen by the passenger door; wireless codes were scrawled over his forehead with a black marker. On the driver side was a picture of King Sihanouk superimposed onto a flower with the words, 'I love my King' printed at the bottom. A fake cactus and a Buddha sat on the dashboard, and two fake monkeys hung off the windscreen mirror.

"Dad, do you think the driver has all these things around him because he is lonely?" Rueben asked.

"Dad the wireless code isn't working. Can you read it to me to make sure I got it right?" Carrie asked.

"Dad I'm hungry," Evan stated.

Mary and I looked at each other and laughed. It was going to be a long journey.

We drove along straight roads, and within a few minutes of watching out the window, I noticed we passed a series of three-wheeled tractors crawling along. One carried swollen sacks of rice, another transported heavily lacquered chairs and beds that looked suitable for a giant and another moved two enormous concrete storm pipes. Next came a motorcycle dragging a caravan-sized market stall with buckets, baskets, dolls and pans tied neatly to the sides. Then we overtook a utility truck carrying chickens in various states of health ranging from fully alive and squawking, to fully dead. The chickens were strung up to all areas of the vehicle including the wing mirrors, and made it look like it was dressed up as an owl and ready for a pageant. Despite this freak show of motor vehicles, everyone shared the road quietly and amicably and it was a great time to people watch.

On the first part of the journey, we endured twenty minutes of an Asian action movie blaring from the television. The film involved people being killed by a pack of well-thrown playing cards that spliced the bad people irreparably. The next film was called 'Dog Eat Man'. I knew this because the opening title was strangely subtitled, but after that it was all in Khmer. The film was a comedy about a rabid dog that terrorised a group of hapless locals. At one point, all the locals jumped into a water hole to escape the dog, but the dog tried to pull down a telegraph pole to drop a mains cable into the water and electrocute them. There was a lot of blood and gore, but that moment of electrocution by a crazy dog got the biggest laugh.

As we entered Phnom Penh, huge puddles lay on the road from an afternoon shower. We sat in a traffic jam outside a petrol station and watched an old lady clear a gutter to allow the water to run off. As she swept at the litter, a large cockroach darted out of the black and muddied mound of refuse.

"Grim!" Carrie spat out.

"Welcome to the capital, Carrie!" I said.

It took another hour to travel the final few kilometres. We crawled along roads crammed with motorbikes and remorks to get to our stop. The total journey took most of the day, but for five dollars, there was no way the journey was going to happen quickly.

As the energy-sapping heat began to wane, we finally reached our hotel. The first thing we did was change into swimmers and head to the pool in the courtyard. For much of the swim, we played a game that

Rueben invented called 'squidgy hands'. It involved creeping up to a family member under the water and squeezing their buttocks or thighs. I never played the game when non-family people were in the pool in case of mistaken identity or an unintended pinch.

After the swim, I sat and wrote at a table outside our room on the third floor. The roar of the city traffic was always heard, but the small pool and foliage in the hotel courtyard provided a little oasis, and a faint smell of barbecue blew in on the breeze. It rejuvenated and dried me.

In the evening we ate at the Cambodia-Vietnam Friendship Monument. The monument was as high as a three-storey house and looked like an ornate dart with a colourful warhead on top. It sat in a vast marble covered square with ornate ponds, dancing fountains and disco lights for company.

We ate dinner from a street vendor whose stall was a side car on a motorbike. For the first time I looked in detail at the motorbikes attached to the stalls. This one was a filthy oil-stained Honda with seats so worn that the springs were exposed. The dinner was delicious though; noodles with a chicken's foot and a perfect amount of chilli.

On the vast marble square that surrounded the monument, locals sat at picnic tables or danced in rhythm to local pop tunes in an organised dance that looked a little like country line dancing and a little like Zumba. We stood and watched them for several songs.

"The men look so camp!" Carrie laughed.

The men danced with such serious faces, as if they were quaffing a fine wine. Unlike in the UK where many men generally dance if they have drunk huge amounts of alcohol or want to impress a potential lover, in Cambodia the men had no such scruples and pulled off shoulder roles and pelvic thrusts that would leave pole dancers in awe. Just one man was not in synch. He danced slightly away from the crowd and had no idea about the moves but waved his arms and hopped from foot to foot in unbridled and carefree joy. If I was dancing, I would look a little like that man.

"Go on Dave – join in," Mary whispered in my ear.

"No," I paused. "I'm worried I'd be too good," I responded.

@@@@@

The next day was the long-awaited shopping day. It was by far the easiest day to get the children ready and Carrie was particularly happy. Our first stop was the Russian Market; the Western name for a market area once popular in the 1980s with expatriate Soviets.

Russia and Cambodia have always had a strong relationship. When the Khmer Rouge was pushed out by the North Vietnamese, there were almost no doctors in Cambodia; most were murdered by the brutal regime. Russia and Cuba were key countries that stepped in to provide medical services in those early years of recovery.

The Russian market looked like an enormous tin shack crammed full of different speciality areas. Under the hot tin roof, the clothes and souvenir section felt oppressing to me, but none of the other family members seemed to notice. We purchased school bags and t-shirts. The school bags lasted a few weeks into the term, but the t-shirts are still worn. Evan insisted I purchase a blue rock that looked suspiciously like plastic, but to him it was treasure. Mary told me to just buy it and reminded me how patient the children were when I wanted to look around the ancient Khmer temples and landmine museum.

In the butcher's area we saw fish get decapitated and chicken bone shards fly, eels slithered across silver trays and crabs sat in aerated pools of water looking a little drugged.

"This is more like it!" I said as we wandered through. The rest of the family crossed their arms hoping to avoid bits of flesh that flew from the machetes.

Phnom Penh: market scene

After a rest and a swim at the hotel, we decided to go to the Royal Palace. It was walking distance from our hotel, but the afternoon was so hot that I caved into my children's demand and agreed with a young driver called Poeu to take us in his remork. Poeu spoke excellent English and explained that he acted as hotel security by night and a remork driver for tourists at the hotel during the day. He did not smile or laugh like many of the drivers, but he was gentle and eager to please.

Poeu looked at Mary as she disembarked outside the palace gates.

"Ah, you will not be allowed in," he said.

Mary wore a short top with exposed shoulders and the Royal Palace was considered a holy temple where all visitors were expected to have their shoulders covered.

"Oh no," Mary said.

"Here, take this."

Poeu went rifling through the cavity underneath one of the passenger seats and pulled out a picnic blanket. He lifted it to his nose. "I'm so sorry. It is a bit smelly."

He almost smiled as he spoke.

"Oh, don't worry, that's really kind," Mary responded, grateful that he could provide her with something.

Even a shawl was not good enough, though, and Mary was forced to purchase a t-shirt that Carrie used for some months afterwards as a night shirt.

So that we would get the best out of the palace, we hired a guide with a drawling and soft American accent that made him sound a little like TV chef Lloyd Grossman.

We walked down a passageway and onto a drive that led to the Royal Palace. It was a magnificent building with roof tiles the same colour as a wasp and ornate pinnacles that looked like building spires from a science fiction film. As we climbed the steps to look into the palace, our guide told us that the king never married.

"Why?" I asked.

"He was too busy to find a wife as he had a career as a ballet dancer in Paris when he was young."

I was impressed he did ballet. I was used to the English royal family where kings in waiting became helicopter pilots for injured people, ran a charity and took long holidays.

"Does the king still dance now?"

Our guide laughed.

"No, he is now in his sixties," he paused. "He may dance privately though. You know the king is from a line of entertainers. King Sihanouk, his father, directed and starred in several movies."

We stood at the edge of a roped-off area and looked into the throne room; squinting at busts made of solid gold and a single throne that was sat on once in a lifetime at a coronation.

"Now we will enter – ", he paused as if adding an effect, "The Silver Pagoda!" Our guide introduced it in a way that sounded a little like Darth Vader and a little like a quiz show host.

Rueben and the Silver Pagoda

The building is known as the silver pagoda because of the silver tiles that cover the floor. Unfortunately, mass tourism meant that the tiles were covered by carpet to protect against the hordes of visitors armed with feet. However, the religious figurines inside were beautiful works of art even though many were missing their heads. Our guide said they were all chopped off by the Khmer Rouge in their desire to wipe out religion.

After an afternoon thunderstorm, we sat at the back of the Silver Pagoda next to a fish pond that was set up as a miniature version of Angkor Wat. Rueben spent much of the time with the fish and followed his favourite one (it had red and black patches) around the pond for many minutes. Carrie and Evan sat with their heads in their hands looking forlorn and considered following fish around a pond about as pointless as painting funny faces on the numerous cockroaches that scarpered in the bushes around them.

@@@@@

The following morning, Mary and I sounded like coffee percolators as we hissed and pushed out watery diarrhoea. Evan also suffered from a sore throat and ear. Only Rueben and Carrie appeared to be fully operating. We started the day a little slower. Carrie withdrew from general awareness of what was happening around her by staring at her phone screen and wearing headphones with the volume turned so high we had to shout at her to be heard. Mary made Evan gargle on salt water though in truth he sounded like he was choking, and Rueben watched cartoons about creatures that look like blueberries.

At breakfast we chatted with the owner of the hotel. She spoke fluent English with a heavy Cambodian accent. We chatted about eating in street stalls and being a little unwell, and about Rueben who ate noodles but did not like too much chili. I thought the owner said, 'too much chilli is a fire in the cellar'. This struck me as jargon for the morning after effect of chilli and considering the morning we had, had so far, I thought it apt. As we dressed after breakfast, I laughed and told Mary how much I liked the expression 'fire in the cellar,' and was praising the woman for her original euphemism for bowel movements post chilli ingestion.

Mary laughed, "Dave, she said, 'fight the seller'!' not 'fire in the cellar'. She meant you have to fight the seller to ensure they do not use too much chilli - the seller of the noodles!"

@@@@@

When the Khmer Rouge rolled into Phnom Penh in 1975, they took over a high school, punched through the classroom walls to make access easier and built cells the size of a train toilet using breezeblocks. They then imprisoned, tortured and murdered over twelve thousand people at the school. Only seven prisoners survived this ordeal. As the bodies began to mount at the converted school, a site needed to be found where the prisoners could be taken, murdered and dumped.

In the morning, Poeu drove us thirty minutes out of Phnom Penh and to the village at Choeung Ek and the pitted field that was chosen for this purpose. 'The Killing Fields' is arguably the most famous monument to the atrocities of the 1970s and the place is beautiful as a remembrance and heart-breaking in equal measure. All of us except Rueben took a headset and audio player and spent three hours wandering around the ditch-ridden grounds.

We listened to stories from guards, local villagers and families who were torn apart by the genocide, and heard accounts about the guards' use of hammers, bamboo poles and the fronds from palm leaves to kill people. The palm leaves were used to cut the throats of the victims so that their screams would not alarm the local villagers. There were lots of people there but because most had headsets, when I removed the headset (something I did so Rueben could hear some of the less gruesome stories), only the wind and birds in the trees were heard.

Rueben held my hand when we got to perhaps the most poignant part of 'the Killing Fields'. On the trunk of one tree, thousands of bangles and bracelets hung as a mark of respect for the children whose brains were bashed out against the trunk. The Khmer Rouge soldiers killed them by swinging the children hard against the tree and then throwing the bodies into a nearby ditch.

"Dad why are there so many bracelets on the tree?" Rueben asked.

I did not know what to say. I told Rueben that there were remains of women and children in the pit but lied about the purpose of the tree and why there were so many bracelets. I said that the tree was a memorial for those who were murdered here. I found it hard to sound calm as my throat tightened in sorrow, and I hoped Rueben would not pick up on the fact that I held back tears. I needed to sit down, though I told him it was because I was hot.

The cruelty of the Khmer Rouge was laid bare to us that day. They used slogans like 'better to kill an innocent by mistake than spare an enemy by mistake," and, "to dig up the grass one must also dig up the roots." This second saying refers to the Khmer Rouge killing off entire families (including babies) to minimise the chances of revenge.

As we wandered along walkways, I saw human bone and rotten cloth half exposed in the ground. Such sights are common in 'the Killing Fields' particularly in the wet season (the time we visited) as the dirt is washed away. At the end of the tour, we entered the mausoleum that rose thirty-five metres into the air, with seventeen levels that house skulls and larger bones of many who were killed.

Having passed skeletal remains washed-up in the dirt and displayed in the monument, I was worried about the effect this experience had on Rueben. I asked him how he found the skeleton remains. He looked confused.

"Well, I walked in there and just saw them," he answered as he pointed at the mausoleum.

I laughed when I realised my inane question and his innocent response but took comfort that he did not appear traumatised.

The tree covered in bracelets at Choeung Ek

After 'The Killing Fields', we travelled onto the S-21 prison. This was the school that the Khmer Rouge converted into their slaughter house. Evan was now struggling with his sore throat and felt sick, and Carrie and Rueben waned in the heat. Mary and I managed to see only three of the five blocks, which was a shame because we found the place fascinating.

When the Khmer Rouge were defeated in Phnom

Penh, there were just fourteen prisoners left at the prison. Rather than just run away, they beat the shackled prisoners beyond all recognition. Even the battle-hardened Vietnamese army were shocked at the mess they discovered. For historical record, the bloodied blobs were photographed to show the world that the reports that came from Cambodian refugees were true. Before that, the world authorities thought the Khmer Rouge was great to support. They even had seats on the UN council and were welcomed by the UK and US.

We passed through rooms full of photographs of prisoners with a board and a number hung around their neck. In the prison, the people had no name, no gender and were referred to as 'it'. Being an individual was not permitted. Some of the people in the photos looked no older than ten years of age. Strangely absent in all photos was any sense of fear. No one ever had tears running down their face and some even looked defiant. Of all stories, and faces that I remember, the one that struck me most was that of Kerry Hammill, a New Zealander who accidently sailed into Cambodian waters, was arrested and then interrogated in the belief that he was a spy. Under interrogation, Kerry told his captors that he was indeed a CIA spy, probably because he was so worn down. Though he did have a joke at the expense of his captors by telling them his boss was Colonel Sanders (the founder of KFC) and poignantly, that his commanding officer was E Star – a reference to his mother whose name was Esther.

Later that day I sat on the balcony of the hotel, drank coffee and read the full transcript that Rob Hammill (Kerry's brother) gave at a tribunal and trial of a former Khmer Rouge leader. He told the court that the family had no news about his brother for over a year, that two birthdays and a Christmas came and went with no news. When the news finally broke, they found out that Kerry had been murdered by reading about it in a newspaper.

No government authority came forward to spend time with the family before the news was made public.

For the second time that day my throat tightened. In his testimony, Rob described the devastation this murder had on his family. Two years after Kerry's disappearance, Kerry's brother John committed suicide having fought a deep depression after the loss of his close friend and brother. At work, his Dad struggled to function, and the successful family business went into decline. Rob described that over the next few years, he often sat and watched television in the living room and heard his Dad in the kitchen doing chores; quietly weeping. His Mother withdrew from life in the community and Rob drank heavily from the age of fifteen to numb the pain. Against the odds, though, Rob picked himself up and went on to become a champion rower and New Zealand politician. Unlike at the tree earlier in the day, I let tears flow freely.

After the visit to S-21, we drank coffee on the back of the remork owned by Poeu. The young driver pulled out some Wikipedia papers he had printed about opposition leaders and spoke with me about the current political situation in Cambodia. The young man wanted to see change in Cambodia and reported that the current opposition leader would declare civil war if the opposition Cambodian People Party did not win power in the next election.

He told me about the opposition leaders who spoke up against the government and had been killed for their views. In July 2016, a prominent political activist Kem Ley was assassinated whilst drinking coffee at a petrol station in Phnom Penh. A week before he was asked to comment on a recent report about the Cambodian leader's family and their vast wealth. In April 2012, Chut Wutty an environmentalist, was escorting two reporters near a forest that he claimed was being illegally logged by the military when he was shot dead. In 2002 Chea Vichea was a trade union activist who had recently started a trade union in a garment factory when he too was shot dead. Speaking out against the establishment was clearly a dangerous activity.

However, Poeu spoke openly about his frustration and did not care who heard him since he had nothing to lose. His voice got louder as he grew in confidence in the conversation, and I looked around at the local people passing by and felt nervous for us and him, in case anyone reported his actions. Judging by the recent Cambodian history we had just read about, we travelled back through the streets of Phnom Penh thinking that there could well be another kick-off if Poeu's desire for change was common.

That evening we ate delicious curry soups at a restaurant across the road from the Cambodia-Vietnam Friendship Monument. We were given a bowl of spicy chicken soup and then given a tray of beans, chillies, flowers and herbs that we picked and added to the soup to enhance the flavour. As I had no idea about the flavour from each herb and flower on the tray, I just added petals and herbs without caution. I could not tell you if it made the soup nicer or not. Rueben had chicken soup where the chicken was butchered by splintering the bones with the meat. I ate his chicken as he complained about bone shards that kept stabbing the top of his mouth, but he ate the broth and noodles. Carrie refused to eat but gave no reason. Mary said it was because she was thirteen and full of hormones.

After dinner, I dropped the family at the hotel and then strolled up to the main road. This was my last evening in Phnom Penh and was the last time I could soak up the atmosphere of the capital city. All along the street, the downstairs rooms of the houses were lit and open to enjoy the evening breeze. In most of the houses, the walls and floors looked grimy and worn through exposure to cooking and city life, and flat screen televisions hung on walls; playing Cambodian soap operas. Some rooms were converted kitchens that served noodles and soup to punters sitting in picnic chairs on the pavements, and many had hammocks strung up where children swayed and stared into their mobile phones. Cars and remorks puttered and sat patiently, head to tail in a queue waiting to get out onto the main road. It was a busy but typical evening street scene in Phnom Penh, and it was far from the vision that the Khmer Rouge had of turning the country into a self-sufficient farming community with no reliance on technology. To me, people seemed content with their lives. I thought about Poeu and his frustration and wondered if I was really witnessing the calm before the storm.

Chapter 4: Kampot and Kep

On the bus ride out of Phnom Penh, Carrie sat in front of me and drew beautiful sketches of flowing hair using a black biro. Rueben sat next to her and drew pictures of fireworks and space and labelled the objects he drew (earth was spelt 'urth'). Each picture Rueben drew took a little over a minute to finish before it was ripped out of his pad, folded up and placed into a new blue bag he purchased a few days before at the Russian Market. Carrie's drawings took far longer.

The bus felt empty as we left Phnom Penh, with only a few locals and a group of Western tourists travelling with us. Five minutes after departing, an older Western couple went to the driver and requested that the television showing Cambodian pop videos be turned down. Across the aisle from me, a young child rubbed his fingers up and down a balloon and made a sound that was half tight fart, half creaking door. A male European traveller sat in the chair in front and had his eyes closed, hoping to sleep off what looked like a hangover. The child continued rubbing the balloon for five minutes and made the hangover man grimace. In the end, the hangover man turned around, gave the child a hard stare and then found another seat at the back of the bus.

I looked out the window, but the view would have done little to improve the grumpiness I had just witnessed. The land between Cambodia's capital city and the coast seemed immense and flat with only a few limestone hills. Some of them looked like hairy pimples and were the only things that interrupted a vista of paddy fields and marshlands. On the roadside, stray dogs wandered around the dusty hard-shoulder, and deserted corner shops lined the roads.

After an hour of travelling through this insipid scenery, thick clouds rolled in and by the time we saw the Cambodian coast for the first time, squally rain pelted the window. I was glad to still have more time on the bus as the rains reminded me of parking-up in expensive carparks at English beaches and eating summer picnics inside the car to shelter from the inclement weather. This was not the climate I imagined I would see in South-East Asia. At the time, I did not know that the rain would only let up intermittently for short periods over the next few days.

@@@@@

'Kampot! I always wanted to visit Kampot since I was sure it was a place Indiana Jones visited in the Temple of Doom.'

Just after I wrote this sentence in my diary, I thought I would do a quick check on the internet and discovered that Indiana Jones went to Pankot and not Kampot. I was disappointed in my confusion.

The bus deposited us on a wide street and just behind an enormous statue of a durian fruit in deference to the excellent crops that grew nearby. One food writer once described the smell of the fruit as "its odour is best described as turpentine and onions, garnished with a gym sock". Every time I saw it for sale, though, I never really noticed its famed malodourous stink.

We took a remork to a local shop to purchase some supplies since we knew that the hotel we booked was a few miles out of town. I stood behind an older European lady with grey and unkempt hair who I guessed may be German. To my surprise, she spoke fluent Khmer to the shopkeeper. As we drove off, I had my first look at Kampot and noticed that the place was full of Western style pizzerias and German bakeries, and there was very little litter lying around.

The hotel was at the end of a dirt road peppered with flooded potholes. I chose the place because it had a pool and was situated on the banks of a river. As we drove in, the surroundings looked beautiful and I expected great things.

The reality was not quite what I expected.

An Italian woman aged in her thirties greeted us as we entered. I thought she was a guest at first; she looked like a backpacker.

"Welcome, I am the receptionist of the hotel," she said.

She reminded me of a curt PE teacher who tolerated very little nonsense.

She suddenly broke off from speaking with us and had a conversation with a cleaner; a Cambodian who bowed after receiving her instructions. I thought the cleaner looked miserable and assumed the receptionist regarded conversations with the staff as more important than speaking with paying guests.

"You are in the beautiful river room. You need to pay for your room in full upfront," she said as she looked at our booking.

This was the first time in South-East Asia that I came across request for payment upfront. It was also the first time in South-East Asia where I was served by a European. Irked but not wanting to cause a scene, I smiled and paid up. As I walked across the gardens to the room, I thought about the Western woman at the shop who spoke fluent Khmer, the suspiciously clean roads, the Western eating places and the Italian receptionist. There seemed to be very few locals. It dawned on me that the place had a significant expat community.

The Italian receptionist was correct. We had a lovely room overlooking the river and a huge mountain, but I noticed that there were no coffee sachets, only tea. I went back to reception and asked if we could have some coffee sachets.

"No coffee sachets, if you want coffee then you need to buy from the kitchen," the receptionist responded.

I was now irritated.

"So, you take the money upfront and when I ask to supply some twenty cent coffee sachets to my room, you say 'no'?"

I think I took the receptionist by surprise.

"Ah. Correct. I will mention that you complain to the manager when he returns", she responded uncertainly.

"Ok thanks," I suddenly felt embarrassed that I complained about coffee sachets.

I knew I was a little irritated about the hotel setup but surprised myself that I was so vocal about coffee sachets. I sat on the new sofa on a balcony overlooking the river and wondered what riled me so much. It dawned on me that I came to Cambodia to have an experience that was different to something I could have in Europe. To only allow customers to drink posh coffee purchased from the hotel felt like a decision made by a European. To be honest, I felt cheated because, if I knew the hotel I stayed in was owned and run by expats, then perhaps I may have made a different choice. Since I paid up front, though, there was no chance of moving. The children had no such sensitivities and they loved the place, so even if I could move, they would never forgive me for taking such action.

The children jumped into the pool with a scream. Western pop tunes played over the loud speakers

"What woman sings this song?" Mary asked as she doggy paddled over to Carrie.

"Oh Mum – it's Ed Sheeran and he's a man!"

Mary and I looked at each other and laughed. Even

Rueben (who never listened to music) knew the song.

That evening we ate noodles in Kampot market. There were no tourists and only a few locals. It was very quiet, and I was not sure if the market was closing because it was evening, or so early in the evening that it was just opening for food. The children ate instant noodles and beef. I looked around at the market that was scrubbed clean and had none of the grit or swagger of any other place I ate in Cambodia. The only colourful thing around us was a pirate's ship. Here, the fun ride was made to look like a chicken with an oversized head that smiled maniacally. I missed the noise, quality food and people-watching at the friendship monument in Phnom Penh.

The following day we woke up to steady rain of the type that I once encountered for a week in Cornwall. On that holiday, it was so constant that I swore never to camp in Cornwall again. Unlike Cornwall, however, the temperature never dipped below twenty-five degrees and so we swam in the rain and splashed out three dead frogs from the pool water. They quickly swelled up in the heat on the poolside; much to Rueben's fascination.

After a few hours, I felt desperate to escape the confines of the hotel and so we borrowed bikes and escaped just as the rains began to slow. We cycled down a wet road and our thighs were quickly spattered in mud. Rueben sat on Mary's bike and Evan sat on mine. As we cycled over bumps, Evan screamed half in laughter and half in tears as each jolt sent stabbing pains into his buttocks. Just before we turned around to go back to the hotel, I investigated the root cause of Evan's yelping and realised that one of the bars of the panier holders that Evan sat on had sheared off. Each time I went over a bump, his left bottom cheek was speared. Still, it was nice to get amongst paddy fields and small children waving at us again, and away from the irritation I felt towards the hotel.

The rain and heat made me itch but finally in the evening, the temperature became bearable and the clouds lifted. It should have made me happy, but I was still irritable as we took a remork into the town. The only plan we had was a visit to a bakery and to eat expensive bread. This was not a plan that excited me. Rueben was tired, and Evan still suffered from a sore throat and saw little point in visiting a town to 'wander around' and 'soak up the atmosphere'. With my struggle to like Kampot and the area, I agreed with him.

Mary and Rueben cycling after a monsoon shower

In the town I started to hum.

"I know you are irritated when you hum," Mary said.

"I'm fine." I responded.

"No, you're not".

"I'm fine."

I thought that with my comment I had won the conversation.

"I know you're not or you wouldn't be humming."

"Hello tuk-tuk?" A driver asked in hope as he drove up and parked right next to us. I shook my head.

"I'm not irritated," I responded.

"Hello – tuk-tuk?"

Another driver stopped by again. This one blocked our path.

I turned to Mary, "how many times do I have to say I'm not irritated?"

I was irritated.

We found a kiosk that sold us watery iced coffees and then we sat by the riverside and watched an armada of fishing boats pass us by with engines that sounded like tractors. With the velvet green hill as a backdrop, it was a beautiful scene and one that finally put me in good mood.

Afterwards, we wandered down streets looking at the faded old shutters and honey coloured houses with corrugated tin rooves. I think I finally began to like the place. I found it easy to spot buildings owned by expats because they had stupid Western names like 'The Dusty Door Knob', 'Roger and the Greek' or 'Kevin's Burger Bar' and there was usually an oversized pot-plant placed by the shop entrance.

As we walked, a little girl barely higher and slightly heavier than a tennis racket ran towards us. To Rueben's surprise she did slow down and ran into his arms for a cuddle. Ruben blushed. Her mother followed a few steps behind, chasing her and holding a spoonful of rice. The mum smiled at us but spoke no English as she lifted her arm and showed us her muscles indicating that the little girl kept her strong. The little girl embraced us all and then followed us down the street like a little puppy. I saved her on several occasions as she tried to climb down off the curb and onto the road on her hands and knees.

She was a lovely and sweet girl who charmed us all.

We ate seafood and Kampot pepper with rice that evening at a street stall. I chatted with the man who cooked for us. He told me that his children (a new born baby and a five-year-old) who swung in a hammock next to the kitchen often slept on the street whilst he and his wife cooked. He said they did have a home but rarely used it. I looked up at the tarp held above us with a mix of bamboo and scaffolding poles and wondered what life must be like living in a makeshift kitchen. I guessed they ate well because the food was delicious. I asked him what his name was. He pointed at the sign tied to a pole by the road. The sign said, 'Smiling Mr. Lok'.

@@@@@

The following day we took a remork to a local beauty spot called Phnom Chhnom cave, about eleven kilometres from Kampot. The mud ochre-coloured road out to the cave went through stunningly beautiful Lincoln green coloured paddy fields. Traditional wooden houses on stilts stood dotted around on islands amongst the growing rice. We passed shops where the owners dozed in hammocks, piglets foraged on the roadside, chickens scraped around in the damp brush, and people passed us on motorbikes; staring and smiling at us and carrying anything from full grown pigs to rice plants.

Our remork stopped and immediately we were greeted by a teenager who introduced himself as Bo. Bo had an air of authority about him and asked me what Khmer words I knew. I was a little taken back and under pressure, all the words I knew fell from my brain. It was like his presence was a cranial enema. With my dumb response, he started teaching us some rudimentary Khmer and pressed me to say 'hello' to the person who sold us the entrance ticket. I suddenly knew how my children felt when they were forced to say 'goodbye' and 'hello' to distant relatives when they visit.

We climbed up the steps and admired views over paddy fields and strips of cabbage and salad that Bo often said were pilfered by the monkeys. At the top of the hill and just before we entered the cave, there was a rustle in the treetop and a tribe of moneys appeared. We stood and watched them from only a few metres away and listened to their gentle calls to each other.

The guidebook raved about the walk up the three hundred steps up the mountain and into a cave with a Cham temple inside and so I was expecting something stunning. If it was food, then I was expecting a fine sea bass. However, all I saw was a damp brick room the size of a garden shed with a rounded stalagmite inside that doubled up as a lingam. The temple inspired me as much as a fish finger.

We climbed down through a small hole in the side of the large cave entrance where at times bright sunlight shone in through collapsed cave ceilings. Bo expected us all to follow him. However, when Mary and I saw that we needed to climb down boulders the size of small cars, we thought one slip would probably result in an injury to a child's brain that could leave it looking like a dropped blancmange. With that thought, Rueben and Mary turned back. Neither were too disappointed, and I think Evan wished he had joined them as we clambered up and down jagged rocks with drops of many metres. I wanted to cry in fear, but Evan came closest to breaking and I needed to steady his shaking buttock with my hand as he wobbled over the rocks.

At the end of the cave, we swung from banyan tree roots like Tarzan. Evan refused to give it a go. Both Carrie and I missed the landing spot and ended up swinging over a ten-metre ledge and required a rescue from Bo. With my inability to remember any Khmer and my lack of coordination to swing from one place to another, he must have thought we were the village idiots on tour.

On the way back, we asked our driver to take us for an iced coffee. He stopped outside the shop where we met the little girl from the previous night. Almost immediately the mother emerged and sat the little girl next to Mary. Our driver told us the girl's name was Lin. We drank delicious strong iced cold coffee while Lin cuddled up to Mary and looked like she was falling asleep.

That afternoon we wallowed by the pool and ate at the same roadside stall run by smiling Mr. Lok. The sun almost came out and with it were butterflies who made their back ends look like heads, and a huge flying green thing that looked like a leaf. I recall one dead frog in the pool and I took that to mean that the weather must be improving.

@@@@@

The following morning, Evan and I hired a kayak from the resort and paddled a few kilometres upstream and into a tributary where the fronds of palms created a natural tunnel and star-shaped water coconuts sat in the mud. On the way out to the tributary, the sky was cloudy, and it rained, and so we were kept cool for the hard part of the paddle. However, I was a fool to think I would not require sunscreen and by the end of the expedition, I carried a raspberry-coloured line across my thighs.

In one quiet and lovely part of the tributary, I saw a small opening that was like a roof of curving leaves growing out of the oily mud. We decided to paddle towards it. Suddenly my stomach cramped up and judging by the gurgling that came from near my bellybutton, I knew I faced the unfortunate choice of pooing my pants and allowing my bowel waters to flow freely through the kayak, or to scramble ashore into the mud and fronds and let forth on the oily bank.

"Evan don't look!" I told him as I scrambled ashore. Clenching and disembarking at the same time was a difficult task.

I told him not to look for his own sake, not mine. However, curiosity got the better of him. I let forth some of the most spectacular and malodorous diarrhoea I have ever had. I had no idea I kept so much water inside of me.

"Oh Dad! That smell! Please let's get out of here! Quick, come on!" Evan screamed and wretched, begging me to get him away from this beautiful corner that I had left badly soiled.

We passed worn out boats parked in the fronds, some sat half capsized in the muddy waters. Evan paddled but got tired easily and often let his paddle drag in the water making us quickly turn in an unintended direction. My outpouring, the effort of paddling a kayak for three hours and the tropical weather (cloud, rain and blazing sunshine) left me barely able to climb back to shore. I felt like I had mild flu. My legs ached, my head ached, and I wanted to sleep.

That evening we sat on a boat moored on the river by an old French colonial bridge and drank cold beer, Caluah and Sprite. We sat on the deck and watched the same flotilla of fishing boats we saw the previous night chug past us for a night of fishing, just like we did on the first night in Kampot. They were all painted the same; red cabins, white stripes and green hulls and I though they looked beautiful in the sunset. I clenched hard as the boats passed so I could enjoy the spectacle, but as soon as they passed, I dove downstairs on the boat and unloaded into a toilet.

"Was there any toilet paper?" Carrie asked as I sat down gingerly again on the deck.

"No," I responded.

"So how did you clean yourself?" Carrie asked.

"I don't want to talk about it," I mumbled.

Mary laughed, and Carrie kept pressing me for an answer.

"It involved a cup of water and an appropriately placed hand."

It was the final evening in Kampot and we ate with smiling Mr Lok for the last time. It took an hour for him to prepare everyone's dinner on a single ring. As I waited, I looked around and next door saw some faded and chipped art deco frescos with the letters E.D.C printed above a door. I asked smiling Mr. Lok what the building used to be.

"Electricity," he said as he smiled and wiped his hands with a rag.

I realised that his stall was set up next to the broken shell of an electricity substation. We sat at a long table and watched him cook and taste the food from the same ladle that he served with. At one point we even saw a rat scurry across the rubble behind his makeshift kitchen, but the seafood amok soup he made us was delicious; coconut, fresh vegetables, squid and unknown local herbs.

In the few hours I spent at smiling Mr. Lok's stall, a few Cambodians on motorbikes drove up and did some business with him but only once did another Westerner eat at his tables. I assumed most visitors wanted to eat at the places with stupid names and pay twenty times the price, which was a shame because despite the unusual surroundings, smiling Mr. Lok was a friendly man and cooked wonderful food. I shook his hand for the last time as I paid him, my family rang out a chorus of thanks, and he bowed reverently as we mutually thanked each other.

After breakfast we took a remork to Kep. As we trundled along the road, the rains suddenly crashed down, and the temperature dropped. Of all the weeks we spent in Asia, it was the very first time we were cold. The driver stopped and pulled down the sides of the chariot to give us protection, but even with them pulled down we shivered and huddled close together. Mary and I sang "Oh I do like to be beside the seaside!" with such gusto that Carrie rolled her eyes and told us that if we do not refrain then she would insist that the driver stop so that she could get out.

Our driver dropped us at a small but stunning resort with a simple pool surrounded by a beautiful garden crammed with banana trees, hibiscus, birds of paradise and other plants that would only be sold as indoor plants in the UK. I was not surprised that Carrie was churlish about our singing, but I was surprised at her reaction when she saw the pool. She clapped her hands and bounced around like a piglet encountering mud for the first time and insisted on a swim without delay. Our daughter seemed to have the ability to veer from miserable to ecstatic within minutes.

The rains still fell from the sky with a gusto rarely seen outside a cyclone and it was cold enough to turn digits blue, but all the children swam. Not surprisingly they shivered when they got out to dry themselves. I felt too middle-aged to feel that uncomfortable and so I sat on soft chairs, played billiards and ate rice whilst we waited for the rains to cease and our room to be made available.

We finally got into the room at two o'clock in the afternoon, a few minutes before a taxi was due to pick us up to take us to see a pepper farm. As I hurried to move our baggage in, Rueben came up to me fully dressed but soaked, and looking like someone just stole his sweets. He explained to me that he was only meant to stick his toes into the water, but he slipped and before he knew it he was fully submerged and fully clothed in the pool water.

"Its OK Rueben. If it wasn't the pool, then you'd probably get soaked by the rains. " I said to comfort my son.

I was pleased to see him strip off and get changed quickly as the taxi was waiting in the forecourt for us. I was also very pleased I dragged him to swimming lessons every Saturday morning.

Our driver to Sothey's farm was a thin gaunt man who smiled a lot and knew some English. He drove through beautiful countryside shrouded in low heavy clouds and past a large windowless building that was constantly playing birdsong.

"Bird's nest soup," he stated as he pointed to the building.

I remember reading about this new farming method for bird's nest soup. Rather than locals risking their lives by clambering up the walls of caves to gather the delicacy, the swifts were encouraged to breed in the windowless building and their nests simply harvested from the building. At three thousand dollars per kilo, this seemed like easy money.

We passed deserted modernist buildings that sat forlorn in enormous puddles. Jungle plants grew on both sides of windows that were framed by crooked shutters hanging from a single rusted hinge. I had no idea what the purpose of the buildings were, but they looked like they were once residential and given the location, would make a fantastic 'fix me up.'

As I thought about this, the driver changed gear and we entered an undulating landscape of sweet potato, pepper and mango plantations. A woman waved at us with a crazy and enthusiastic wave as she sat and watched over her fly-infested cows grazing on the roadside.

At the farm, we were greeted by a guide, a young man who was there to improve his English and tell us about the farm. Three bowls of the different peppercorns they grew were placed on a table for us to taste. We did warn Rueben that it may be hot, but he insisted on tasting a corn and immediately took off running around the muddy forecourt like a man with his pants on fire.

"Water!" he screamed, much to the guide's delight.

Just after the guide started his presentation, a German family turned up and they struggled to understand the accent of our guide. He described the use of bat droppings as a natural insecticide, but the Germans struggled to understand him. When the German's pressed him to explain the point, he replaced the word 'manure' with 'shit' much to Carrie's and Evan's shock and slight delight.

We learnt there were two types of pepper on a plant; the green and the red. The green peppercorns turned black and were the least peppery in taste. The red ones (once dried) had a far stronger kick but could be boiled and skinned to make them white.

At one point on the tour of the farm, we entered a shed where we saw men armed with tweezers hunched over a plate of peppercorns; separating the red from the black. I cannot imagine a job more tedious than sifting through peppercorns. As I looked at those workers, I made a mental note that whenever I want to encourage my children to work hard at school I should remind them that if they do not get the grades they need, they could end up sifting peppercorns for a job.

@@@@@

Kep became a town in the early 1900s and spent seventy years as the top beach resort for the elite of Phnom Penh. In the 1970s, the Khmer Rouge put an end to recreation and left the place to rot. When we visited, the area still did not feel like a town and the places to eat along the beach looked expensive and spartan. We asked the driver if there were local markets and he kindly took us to a dirt road a few kilometres from the beach that was lined with stalls selling barbecued meat.

There, we put an order on for barbecued seafood kebabs and chicken. As the meat cooked, I noticed a filleted piece of meat about the size of my hand. I saw frog before in markets and so asked if this was a frog. As I asked, I realised there was a small claw on the foot.

"Frog? No," she paused, as if thinking about the word in English.

"Rat," her colleague reached over and said.

Armed with food, we drove a few kilometres to the beach with cool and damp sand and muddy water lapping onto the shore. Tree covered hills towered above us and a few moments of sunshine created enormous shadows out to sea. Locals sat on blankets and enjoyed an evening picnic, and placid dogs roamed around looking for scraps. We sat on Kep beach and ate our chicken and seafood kebabs on beds of boiled rice. My rice came with a tangy tamarind sauce that was disconcertingly crunchy. I imagined I had just placed a bag full of crushed fish bones over my rice and it was not at all pleasurable.

"Oh, my goodness – it still has fur around the bottom!" Carrie screamed out as she examined her chicken.

Most of her dinner went to a stray dog at Kep beach. A few months later she declared herself a vegetarian and I strongly suspect that this discovery of fur on her chicken was a significant moment that put her on that path.

After dinner we walked to the crab market (the crab market is a small commercial hub on the outskirts of Kep with a basic market and row of ramshackle restaurants about a mile from the beach) along a curvy road that hugged the coast line. Water crashed against the sea wall on one side and monkeys played in the trees and street signs on the other.

Hidden in the bushes were old bungalows covered in graffiti, algae and vines. They belonged to the rich and the famous of Phnom Penh but had sat empty since the 1970s when the Khmer Rouge rolled into town.

As we walked, stray dogs sat huddled next to tree trunks, and monkeys scavenged in the gloom along the sea walls. It was dark when we arrived at the crab market. We would have got there much quicker and possibly even in daylight had Evan not walked so slowly; complaining about chaffing after his shorts got wet on Kep beach. Rueben also walked reluctantly as he complained he was tired and threatened to sit on the curb and spend the night with the monkeys.

@@@@@

In the morning, the sun came out and the children went straight to the pool. Everyone shrieked as a great gurgle heralded the arrival of the bubbles in the hot tub. It must have done something to the filter because a great bomb of algae turned the pool water a tinge of green within seconds. No wonder I woke up that morning with an earache.

With the sun finally out, we made our way to the beach. The sunshine seemed to be winning in an uneasy battle with a storm, but a wind that whipped up the sand on Kep beach and stung our skin was a reminder that rain was never far away. In the distance, banks of clouds hung over the jungle covered Phu Coc Island that sat a few miles out to sea. From where we sat on the beach, we heard chains of shells made up as souvenirs smash together as they hung on the makeshift stalls set up by the road.

To swim in the muddy brown waters and escape the stinging sand was lovely. We played in the water and bobbed on the waves for three hours. As waves approached, I heard Rueben screaming regularly, "It's a piggy!" It took me a while to work out what he was saying, but I realised he referred to the approaching waves and the 'P' was in fact a 'B'.

That afternoon we walked from the Kep Crab to the Crab Market. The Kep Crab (basically a concrete crab the size of a small car) in the backdrop of a large storm looked a little vulnerable sitting just offshore. We purchased some honey-flavoured biscuits from a seller walking along the promenade and the children wanted me to do business with vendors that sold ice creams in cones that looked like scrolls. There were street stalls with slices of crab sticks, sausages and instant noodles. And the sight of all the food made Evan feel very hungry.

The sun quickly fell and like the previous evening, the long shadows were everywhere. Within minutes, the single shadow of the mountain behind the beach cast its shadow across the entire beach.

We took the same road to the crab market that we walked the previous day. Even though monkeys played around us, Evan was fully focussed on the impending dinner at the crab market.

"Dad – what are you going to have? I think I'm going to have barbecued shrimp."

"I'm not sure Evan," I responded.

"So, have you made a choice between chips and rice yet?"

"Ah," I paused, "no."

We wandered on with Mary and Carrie chatting away ahead of me, Evan talked at me about the menu and Rueben brought up the rear singing and dancing like a pied piper.

@@@@@

Evan has always loved food and is happiest when it comes regularly and in bulk. Just after we moved back from Australia and were making friends in the UK, Mary and I were excited when Evan was invited for a playdate and tea. At the end of the date, the father dropped off Evan and I thanked him for his kindness. The father laughed.

"Evan really knows how to eat," the father said.

I laughed, "what happened?" I asked.

"He ate more than my wife and I put together. At the end of the dinner he asked for more, and after he ate seconds, he then asked for thirds. I had to say to him, 'There's no more mate, you've emptied the cupboards, I'll have to go back to the supermarket."

"Yeah that sounds like Evan," I responded.

"I haven't finished yet," the father said, "Evan after a few moments turned around and asked me, 'when are you going to the supermarket?'"

Evan was never invited back to that house again.

@@@@@

We ate in a group of restaurants built out over the sea wall. They were basically ramshackle sheds. The restaurant we chose had walls and ceiling covered with palm leaves and it gave us the impression that we were sitting and eating in an enormous basket.

Evan ordered barbecued shrimp, but his world came crashing down when our waiter spoke poor English and translated the word shrimp for squid. Eventually the shrimp arrived, and Mary removed the heads and tails and skin due to Evan's clumsy inability to remove the skin.

I ate crab and broke claws with my teeth and

sucked meat out of tubular bones; covering my mouth and hands in delicious sweet crab curry. I felt and looked like a two-year-old eating Spaghetti Bolognese with red sauce splattered on my cheeks. We all thought our food was a delicious and a lovely finale to our time on the Cambodian Coast.

Most importantly, Evan was satisfied.

Chapter 5: Kampong Chhnang

Our guesthouse in Kampong Chhnang had enormous baroque chocolate-coloured wooden chairs around a picture of the king that looked disturbingly like my boss at work. On the main reception counter was a pen holder with a bucking horse and two dolphins exploding theatrically from each side; all the pens were missing. On the far side of the reception area was an enormous wooden carving of a fish pond that kept us occupied as we counted the fish whilst we waited for our rooms. We think there were nineteen.

The young hostess looked like she had just left school and perfectly matched these surreal surroundings, because she spoke English with a confidence and a smile that exuded a message that I should understand her. However, she spoke with a delightfully thick accent that I found impossible to decipher.

I had no idea what she asked and stood there unsure what to say, wishing for the second time in a few days that I had put more effort into learning some Khmer. Mary, with her years of work with small children, jumped in to help.

"We want a room with air-con," Mary responded.

It was early afternoon when we arrived, and we were all hungry, and so decided to walk along the main highway to the local market.

"Can I stay here at the hotel?" Carrie asked.

"No," I responded. "You'll get hungry. We all need to eat."

"But it's going to rain," she said

"No, it's not," I responded.

"Yes, it is."

"No, it's not."

"Yes, it is," Carrie responded.

"No, it's not."

"Dad it always rains in the afternoon," she said

"We'll be fine," I responded.

Mary gave Rueben the remains of his breakfast baguette and because he focussed on eating, the walking pace was painfully slow. Kampong Chhnang is not a popular tourist spot and so whilst Carrie, Evan and I stood and sweltered whilst we waited for Mary and Rueben, many people stopped their activities for a good and long stare at us. A group of road workers stopped road repairs and sweeping to have a gawp, and a girl wearing a 'just smile' t-shirt cycled passed at least five times to have a thoroughly good look at us.

"Come on Mary," I mumbled, keeping an eye on the crowds who regarded us as a walking freak show. I wondered if she was walking slowly on purpose since I turned prickly when she asked the receptionist where the market was situated.

"Mary," I snapped, "I know where the market is. It's marked on the map."

In the heat, snapping is never a good thing to do with a well-meaning wife, but I think my mild bickering with Carrie over rainfall possibilities that afternoon probably added to my poor judgement that led to me snap at Mary.

When we finally got to the market, we found two stalls that sold our favourite things. There was a stall with a basket the size of an arm chair that was full of bread, and next door a stall sold iced coffee served in bags. The bread and the coffee soothed our frayed nerves. Rueben received special attention from the motherly stall holders and one stroked his face and gave him a roll. He accepted it with grace, a warm smile and a shy thank you.

As we drank the coffee, dark clouds exploded and

within seconds we huddled under umbrellas that sagged under the weight of the deluge.

Carrie looked at me and scowled, "told you!" she shouted over the noise of torrential rain.

Mary laughed.

Forced deeper into the market, we passed spaces where ladies made clothes on old sewing machines that looked like they should be in museums, and jewellers resized rings. The passageways dripped from the monsoon showers outside and the gutters and drains that were cut along the narrow passageways were full of inky water and soggy cardboard. I avoided the waters with my big manly strides, but the children struggled and had to straddle the streams to move along the aisle. They walked like they had just wet themselves. Closer to the meat area, a cat with bald patches scurried away. We felt trapped and took a few minutes to work out how to escape. The only exit we found was over two sleeping dogs that guarded a lifeless restaurant. Beyond the restaurant, we walked down a narrow alleyway cordoned off with a low chain, and still we needed to watch where we stood as there was mushy trampled fruit lying all over the path.

"This is disgusting," Carrie said, "I should have stayed at the hotel."

Then her heel slipped on a ground-in marrow.

@@@@@

Our reason to come to Kampong Chhnang was to see the nearby floating villages and the local handicrafts. When we got back to the hotel, we asked the receptionist to book a taxi to take us to see the pottery just outside of the town. The receptionist said something I did not understand, but again Mary comprehended.

"Ah. Driver or Guide?" Mary asked as she looked at

me. She did not wait for me to respond.

"Guide as well if possible," Mary said.

I was astounded that my wife was so in tune with this receptionist, and I still had no clue what she said.

We rested in the room for an hour and then the phone rang. I knew why, but I thought it polite to let the receptionist speak. Silence.

"Guide here!" she announced with a joy that reminded me as if it was a mother telling her child, "It's Christmas!"

"Oh Dad, we're not going out again, are we?" Carrie complained.

At the entrance to the hotel, I introduced myself to Mr. Vani. I was surprised when he held out his hand in greeting; no other Cambodian greeted me this way before. I should have been suspicious but there was something about him that made me instantly trust him.

"I learnt English from a retired British soldier who stayed for several months to teach English," Mr Vani shouted over his shoulder as we chatted in the remork.

I suspected this was where he learnt about hand shaking as well. He smiled as he drove and chatted with the children about mundane things like places we have seen in Cambodia and school in England. He reminded me of an ideal uncle.

He drove along dirt roads and into some of the most beautiful Cambodian countryside I encountered, with verdant paddy fields and towering palm trees, uniform in shape.

"Dad they look like thin upside-down toilet brushes," Evan said.

"Like I care," Carrie mumbled under her breath.

Spectacular grey monsoonal clouds cowered low over the vista and battled with the sun. The sun momentarily broke through for a second and then the clouds smothered out the light.

We stopped at a local community business that made pots and charcoal basins used for cooking. The factory was just a sprawling shelter covered in corrugated tin and it sat in the shadows of a mountain called 'Golden Mountain'; named because of the flecks of gold often found in the clay. Lots of different aged people worked there. I saw babies asleep in hammocks; happy next to their mothers. School aged children were also present and packed rice husks around the clay pots to give them a darker appearance once they were fired. Mr. Vani said the children came here to earn some money for books and shirts for school.

Countryside around Kampong Chhnang

Next, we drove and parked up near a typical Cambodian house on stilts. As the engine died on the remork, we heard children singing with an enthusiasm rarely seen outside a football terrace. I realised that the voices came from the church next door. Mr. Vani said the church was run by Koreans.

"The children love coming," he paused, "but only because the Koreans give bags full of goodies as a gift to them all."

The children poured out of the church looking very happy. None of them carried gifts. Almost immediately they cowered in the shelter of the balcony as the monsoonal clouds broke with an enthusiasm I have only ever seen from a burst water main.

We also took shelter, though we ran from the remork to underneath the house. There, a plump and smiling woman sat at a pedal-powered potter's wheel and turned lumps of clay into useful objects. The rain on the tin roof was so loud we needed to raise our voices to be heard. To watch her as she took a clay lump and made it into a cup left us all looking at her as if she were a magician that astounded us with a trick.

"Dad can we have a go?" Rueben tugged on my sleeve.

She laughed and smiled and said something I did not understand to Mr. Vani. Then she beckoned us one at a time to sit down opposite her and gently used our fingers to make a vase or a cup. Rueben went first and bit his bottom lip in concentration as she took his fingers and turned a lump of clay into something beautiful. I took a photo of him holding his creation as he held it next to his febrile looking cheeks. After I took the photo, his shoulders dropped when I told him that it was not possible to carry a wet clay pot away with us.

We drove up muddy roads that were now in full flow and felt thankful that we were protected in the chariot towed by the motorbike, for the rains were unrelenting. After a few minutes and a struggle up a steep driveway, we stopped next to a homestead and ran once more for a sizable communal shelter. The first thing I notice were the snail shells the size of clenched fists that hung on strings hung around the walls. We greeted the owner and Mr. Vani negotiated something in Khmer. Mr. Vani gave us umbrellas and led us then to a shack where I heard a dull thudding that sounded like someone beating a quilt.

Rueben and his pot

A beautiful and gentle woman bowed reverently as we entered and then carried on her beating as Mr. Vani explained that she made pots using traditional Khmer methods. He told us that the woman took a rough mould of a pot, placed it on a straight stump of a palm tree and then beat the clay using a baton in one hand and a wedge held tight against the inside of the drying clay with the other. It took an hour to make a single pot and the woman walked a kilometre in the process.

"These traditional methods, they die in Khmer Rouge day," Mr. Vani said as we watched her walk around the stump and beat the pot. The woman said she created around fifteen pots per day using this method.

We returned to the shelter with the snail shells and sat on plastic chairs and Mr. Vani gave us a lecture about the palm trees with the man who he negotiated with earlier. I tried to listen to the information but something else kept grabbing my attention.

"Mary don't take this the wrong way, but that man looks like a doppelganger of your Dad," I whispered.

"I know I was thinking that as well." Mary responded.

She smiled, and I knew she was thinking of someone close but recently gone. Her Dad died two years before.

We drove through the countryside back to Kampong Chhnang. The storm was gone, but clouds still hung low though they seemed spent and benign. Mr. Vani drove slowly, and I happily photographed the scenery. Everyone else looked a little bored.

"Dave have you finished?" Mary asked, clearly irritated by the slow pace.

"Yeah Dad, come on let's get back to the hotel," Carrie said, supporting her mother.

"Yeah, I could be done," I replied as I took another photo and thoroughly enjoyed the slow pace to take in the view.

"Well if you have finished, can you tell him? I think he is driving slowly because he thinks you want to take photos," Mary responded.

"Nah. He is driving slowly so that he too can enjoy the lovely scenery," I responded as I took another photo.

We went through several more cycles of this conversation before Mary gave up and allowed me to photograph and Mr. Vani to drive slowly for whatever reason he saw fit.

On the way back, Rueben screamed with joy the moment we passed a playground complete with plastic slides and raised platforms. It was the first playground we saw in Cambodia. Mr. Vani was happy to stop, and Rueben and I raced over. The other two children folded their arms and slouched in the remork, obviously seeing this stop as an inconvenient delay to getting back to the hotel.

As I followed Rueben to the playground, I noticed some monkeys were near the remork but did not take too much notice. Suddenly I saw Carrie and Evan leap out of the carriage laughing as if they had discovered a large spider crawling up a leg. I did not race back to see what happened because Mary was with them and I needed to keep an eye on Rueben. However, when I returned, they told me a monkey tried to steal the water bottle. Mary realised just in time and turned to face it; picking the bottle up instantly and raising it to use it as a weapon. The monkey hissed, as did Mary. It happened in a second, but Mary won. She is amazing, I think I would have donated my bottle to the thieving monkey.

That evening we walked through a park in the centre of town in search of a street stall for dinner. The park was covered in frangipanis and pathways. Locals sat on park benches enjoying the balmy damp evening air and children ran around playing chase with their friends. We were probably the only tourists in town and were local celebrities. As we walked, children greeted us, and teenagers giggled behind mobile phones; photographing us as we passed by.

Evan spotted some cooking sausages and demanded we explore no further. I asked for my sausage to come with chilli sauce. After some pointing and smiles, the sausages arrived on a bed of onion shreds. The sausages were delicious, but the chilli sauce was some of the hottest I hadever encountered. It left me in tears and the following morning I suffered with a fire in the cellar.

As I winced from the chilli heat, two young men

beckoned us over and asked if we would share their plastic garden table with them. They spoke in uncertain English; every word had to be thought about.

"Where you from?" one of them asked.

"England," I said smiling, wiping drips off my cheeks.

"Oh England!"

Pause. He was obviously trying to remember some English.

"Where you been?" he asked.

"Battambang, Siem Reap, Phnom Penh, Kep" I listed the places. As I said each one, he repeated the place after me. I paused as I took a tentative bite from the fiery sausage again.

"Do you live here in Kampong Chhnang?" I asked.

"Ah no," he laughed, "here for exam."

He took a sip on his beer.

"You live London?"

"Nearby," I said. "I work in London,"

I paused, "One day you visit?"

"Ah no, no. So much money!" I looked away awkwardly, as did the young man.

I felt embarrassed about asking such a question in this circumstance and was uncertain about what to say next. The young man turned around to the vendor who gave us the sausage, and two iced cold beers were placed next to Mary and me.

"A present," he smiled.

I still felt ashamed but touched by this gesture in equal measure. It should be me buying the beer. I thanked him and smiled as I lifted the beer and took a sip. Two minutes later, he stood up with his friend, said an uncertain goodbye and walked into the crowd.

@@@@@

As a family we saw amazing beaches, temples and ate delicious food. However, it is the kindness of strangers that has touched me the most.

Just after Mary and I met, we travelled around the world. New Zealand was one of our last places to visit and we were running a little low on money. I knew I had some relatives in the country and thought staying with them would save some cash. So, I wrote to my Grandmother to ask about them. She responded a few weeks later with the address of Hilary and John. Hilary was my Dad's cousin and I vaguely remembered meeting her when I had bad acne as a teenager and probably stank of cigarette smoke. I was a bit worried about the reception they would give me considering the reception I probably gave them the last time they saw me.

I need not have worried because from the moment they picked us up at the airport, we felt like we were the centre of their universe. Not only did they provide a roof over our heads, they organised a party of the wider Tucker family members and they paid for us to go and view a surreal exhibition of Antarctica where the highlight was a display of penguins kept in an underground cage. We may have been distant family, but these people were still strangers and they treated Mary and I like royalty. However, there was one simple thing that Hilary did that began a change in my life which is still going on.

The years after Dad died were tough years. I had my finger on the self-destruct button of nearly all my friendships. To my shame, I cared more about being the centre of attention than caring for other people and their feelings. Girlfriends came into my life and usually departed in tears or with a door slam and a curse, and I lost contact with all my university friends as they lost patience with my attempts to be the life of a party that they thought had finished. Looking back, I think my friends grew up, but my growth was a little stunted and I found it difficult to relax, difficult to sleep.

One evening in Auckland, Hilary and I sat up late. She asked a few questions about family life and my life and I did most of the talking. At the end of the evening, she asked if she could pray for me. Praying was something that I had not done for a very long time but as an attendee of church in my youth, her offer was not a strange one to me and I was touched by her kindness as no one dared pray with me for years. That night after she prayed, I had the deepest and most refreshing sleep I have ever had.

It took a few years to happen, but I eventually returned to my Christian faith that I knew as a child, and I have not looked back. I remember that evening with Hilary where my journey back to my Christian faith began. Perhaps the most touching thing about this story is that Hilary cannot even recall the night specifically; to show such kindness was an everyday event to her.

Nearly always the kindness of strangers is small; a prayer or a beer. However, I am always amazed how that kindness touches my soul.

@@@@@

Each monsoon, the Tonle Sap Lake swells to six or seven times its normal size. If the lake was an accordion then it is the equivalent of going from the instrument being pressed together and sitting comfortably in a lap, to the sides being pulled apart to a man's full stretch. Many thousands of people live on the lake in floating villages and one of the main reasons to visit Kampong Chhnang is to visit one of these villages.

The road by the lake was lined with stalls selling

fruit, bread, baskets, mobile phones and scaffolding poles. It bustled with traffic; motorbikes pulled carts loaded with people and goods, and huge trucks weighed down with bulging sacks of rice threw up dust that made us squint. On the side going down to the river, the stalls were built out over the banks with small alleyways leading to the litter-strewn river's edge where longboats sat idle; moored to a single post.

Two ladies with most of their front teeth missing escorted us to the dockside and gave us life jackets to truly mark us out as tourists, much to Carrie's embarrassment. They made us climb into longboats. As I climbed in, the boat rocked violently, forcing me to immediately lay flat as if someone was shooting at us.

"Dad's so embarrassing," I heard Carrie whisper to her mother.

I ignored her, and the boys clambered into my boat. They had no such concern about their Dad.

At first the drivers used the motors to propel us a few kilometres up the river to the floating village. On the flat and mud-coloured waters of the Tonle Sap and in the hazy light, the village from a distance looked lifeless and insignificant.

My first impressions, however, were completely wrong. As we approached the first few houses the drivers cut the engines and started to paddle. We passed rows of ramshackle floating houses that up close were full of colour and life. People sat cross legged; fixing nets and banging bits of metal with hammers. Women combed knots out of their hair, children waved, cats stopped licking between their legs and stared at us, and dogs met us with a tired look from their shoulder at times, at other times with teeth-bearing hostility.

At one point we passed a man and his teenage son eating. Unlike everyone else they did not smile as we went by. He said something to our driver that sounded gruff and staccato. I wondered if he was expressing his displeasure in the fact his town and his life was a tourist attraction. Our diver tutted and did not respond.

As we went around, the children discussed what jobs they would do if they lived on the Tonle Sap. Carrie would be a weaver, Evan would be a fisherman, Rueben said he would be a boat driver and sell fruit. Mary said she would be a nurse and I wanted to be a butcher.

Teeth-bearing dog in the floating village.

We passed boats laden with fruit and other supermarket goods. They did their business by stopping at each floating house for a few minutes. One of the drivers purchased a cold drink and some paracetamol from one of these boats. I was not surprised our driver had a headache because, when the sun came out, it was instantly hotter than the inside of a pan of steamed broccoli, and paddling people around in the heat must have been exhausting.

That afternoon, the rains fell with the same passion we saw on the previous day and Mr. Vani said it was too wet to go into the countryside again as we planned. We thanked him and said goodbye.

After the rains stopped, we went to the local playground we had visited the previous day. Once again, monkeys patrolled the area hunting down food left unattended by parents or children. Each time a monkey moved, the parents scooped up their children and hissed at the primates.

When Rueben arrived, he shot up the stairs and down the tubular slide. Two Cambodian children were clambering up the slide chatting and laughing. As they met Rueben coming down, there was a stunned silence followed by two frightened Cambodian children scampering out the bottom of the tube in shock. After a few minutes though, Rueben made four friends and played tag. In the close heat, they sat down to rest; t-shirts covered in sweat. They were united in play and rest even though they were unable to understand any words each other spoke.

@@@@@

We returned to Siem Reap the following day. After dinner the children went to get a henna painting on their arm as a farewell event. Rueben got an elephant on the underside of his wrist, Carrie got a flower and Evan got a moon. All the children sat down after they were painted, and I told them not to move and smudge the henna. Rueben could not help but move and got a slight smudge on his elephant and was immediately crushed. He tried to hold his emotions together but in the end the tears won. The young woman who did this was so touched by his pain that she repaired his elephant and did another one for good measure on the other wrist to sooth his broken spirit.

Whilst they sat still, I wandered around the old market and came to the fish section. People were packing up, turning out lights and washing away the meat and fish matter from their stalls. Carrie always baulked in these areas, but I found them a wonderful lens into life. I was certain my children and beloved wife would not miss the butcher sections in the markets, but I knew I would. With the sight of them all packing up, I suddenly felt low. Next time they set up we would be on a plane back to Hong Kong.

Early the following morning, we drove back to the airport and looked around at Cambodian street life for the last time; the street stalls, people relaxing in hammocks on the roadside and the motorbikes that choked the roads.

A road scene in Cambodia

"I'm going to miss this place," Carrie said. "A

little," she added the final comment as if to curtail my pleasure in hearing her speak like this.

"I know we are wired a little differently my beloved," I said to her gently. I told her I loved her and kissed her head.

We all continued looking out at the street life. For the first time I recall, none of us had anything to say.

"You never quite know what will be around the corner in places like this." Mary said after a minute.

As if proving this point, a second later, we turned a corner and the driver pulled hard on the brake. We all lurched forward. In front of the vehicle were two immobile dogs stuck together after mating. The boys howled at the sight of the unfortunate dogs. Carrie blushed.

Mary was right. I thought about my Dad again and a life cut short. He did not know what was around his corner and I do not know what is around mine. That is why I took my young family on these adventures, though sometimes I wonder how they will remember them. I hope they remember the kindness of strangers and that they are inspired to be kind in turn. I am sure they will remember the sweat and the hills we climbed, though I hope those memories are peppered with joy. Above all, I hope they also take a few risks and go on adventures themselves in their lives, even if those adventures have a different flavour from mine.

About the book

These adventures to Sri Lanka, Vietnam and Cambodia happened over a three-year period with each country visited for two to three weeks. Travelling with children made me mindful of travelling far off well-trodden tourist paths; partly for safety reasons, but mostly because my children were never keen on very long bus rides! Our pattern of travel was that we stayed in a place for a few days, had day trips out from that place and enjoyed the people and sights that we encountered.

At all times we travelled independently. This is because we believe in making our own adventure and because we want to place our money into the hands of the local people we met.

My children and wife are key characters in the following adventures and agreed to be the protagonists. However, their names have been changed for the sake of their privacy and anonymity. Also, all the people we met and businesses we used have a right to privacy and so names and some characters have been changed unless explicit approval has been given. However, the story is a true and accurate account of our experiences.

Printed in Poland
by Amazon Fulfillment
Poland Sp. z o.o., Wrocław

50582940R00157